Fresh Light

Homilies
on the
Gospels of
Year A

Fresh Light

Homilies on the Gospels of Year A

Joseph Pollard

HillenbrandBooks

Chicago / Mundelein, Illinois

First published in Europe by The Columba Press/55A Spruce Avenue Stillorgan Industrial Park /Blackrock Co., Dublin/Ireland. European edition © 2003 Joseph Pollard. Published by arrangement with the author and publisher.

FRESH LIGHT: HOMILIES ON THE GOSPELS OF YEAR A / NORTH AMERICAN EDITION © 2004 Archdiocese of Chicago: Liturgy Training Publications, 3949 South Racine Avenue, Chicago IL 60609; 1-800-933-1800, fax 1-800-933-7094, e-mail orders@ltp.org. All rights reserved. See our Web site at www.LTP.org.

Hillenbrand Books is an imprint of Liturgy Training Publications (LTP) and the Liturgical Institute at the University of Saint Mary of the Lake (USML). The imprint is focused on contemporary and classical theological thought concerning the liturgy of the Catholic Church. Available at bookstores everywhere, or through LTP by calling 1-800-933-1800 or visiting www.ltp.org. Further information about the **Hillenbrand Books** publishing program is available from the University of Saint Mary of the Lake/Mundelein Seminary, 1000 East Maple Avenue, Mundelein, IL 60060 (847-837-4542), on the web at www.usml.edu/liturgicalinstitute, or e-mail litinst@usml.edu.

15 14 13 12 11   6 5 4 3 2

Printed in the United States of America.

Library of Congress Control Number: 2004110145

ISBN 978-1-59525-004-9

HFFLA

"Above all, it's the Gospels that occupy my mind.
I'm always finding fresh light there."

Thérèse of Lisieux, *Autobiography*

Contents

For John V. Sheridan

I will hold my house in the high wood
Within a walk of the sea.
And the men that were boys when I was a boy
Shall sit and drink with me.

—Hilaire Belloc

Introduction

This is a book of short homilies on the Gospel for the Sundays of
Year A. It includes some solemn days and feasts. It is a departure from
the usual liturgical practice for homilies. Ideally, all three Sunday
readings and the responsorial psalm form a unity, and suggest a common theme for the Sunday liturgy. The homily might be expected
to reflect the theme.

Like other homilists, I have spent many years following this
ideal. Like many of them, I have found that the number and richness
of the readings are a challenge to the homilist who may have, at
most, ten minutes to deal with them. These homilies are based on the
Gospel only.

Each homily begins with the Lectionary reference number
and the Gospel citation. I keep textual explication to a minimum.
For this I am indebted to others, especially the late William Barclay.
I concentrate on the core message and its possible pastoral appli-
cation in our circumstances. The assigned Gospel may vary, depending
on liturgical requirement, but this is an infrequent occurrence. Some
lines in this book appeared in my previously published homilies.

The book follows the premise that there is more than enough
in the Gospel reading alone to speak to our hearts. In addition, there
is something unique about the Gospel. Notwithstanding the fact that
"all scripture is inspired of God and is useful for teaching—for reproof,
correction, and training in holiness" (2 Timothy 3:16), the book of
the Gospels has a pre-eminence in divine revelation and in the liturgy
of the Church. The Gospel is the Church's own best understanding
of who Jesus is and of his relationship with us. As such, it commands
a Christian's best attention and speaks to the very core of his or
her heart. It always will, no matter the generation or the changing
social scene.

Advent

1A First Sunday of Advent

MATTHEW 24:37–44

Be Ready!

Three different events are woven together in this twenty-fourth chapter of Matthew. They are the coming of the kingdom, or God's definitive rule, on earth; the destruction of Jerusalem and its temple; and the second, or final, coming of Christ at the end of time. The event of concern in today's Gospel is the second coming as it is popularly called.

The recent millennium event brought many people face to face with the issue of the second coming of Christ. The world suddenly was alarmed with wild predictions about its nearness. The alarm passed, of course, but many young people asked, for the first time in their lives, what is the second coming? It is the return of the glorified Jesus at the end of time to bring salvation history to a close. It is not meant to be a fearful day for believers; it is meant to be a day of great joy— something, in fact, to look forward to.

Jesus speaks of the suddenness and the unexpectedness of his second coming. We cannot predict its timing. He tells us to be ready for it, to be prepared. Are we?

Our Lord's words suggest that most people will be unprepared. When that day happens, people will be living just another ordinary day in their ordinary lives. For example, they will be in their car on the way to work, or at their desks computing, or having lunch, or in church getting married, or in a cemetery burying a parent, or at home worrying about the mortgage, or watching college football on Saturday afternoons, or having a drink in the neighborhood bar with a few of their friends in the evening. There is nothing wrong with any of that. It's all part of the stuff of our lives. I believe the scriptures generally support the thesis that such is what we should be doing in any event. Our Lord is only suggesting that his final coming needs to be on our minds as the joyful possibility for each day of a Christian's life, no matter what else is on the agenda for the day.

There is an anonymous story about three apprentice devils who tell Satan how they will destroy the faith of earthlings. One says, "I will tell them there is no God." The second says, "I will tell them there is no hell." The third says, "I will tell them there is no hurry." "Go," said Satan to the third one, "and you will ruin thousands." There is no hurry; there is plenty of time!

Perhaps today more than ever, each day's agenda is so crammed with everything but God that the second coming is not even vaguely on our minds. We don't need an apprentice devil to tell us that there's no hurry about being ready for the Lord; the frantic modern world makes sure that we have our minds on everything but the Lord. Is this generation, then, unprepared? If the crammed agenda of each modern day, and the death of the sense of our personal sinfulness, and the sparse numbers at sacramental confession are barometers, the answer has to be yes.

The Lord's observation about being ready to confront the burglar of your house is telling. Our homes are insured, triple-locked, and alarmed to the hilt these days—because all our treasures are in our homes. The treasures are the spouse and the children, of course, but they are also the hard-earned appliances and the art, the artifacts, and the ambience that are normal now in the Western economy. I do not condemn them; they are measurements in our sweat and blood. They represent the many days and years of our hard-working lives. But what of the house of the human heart, the spiritual house of faith? Surely it is to that house that the Lord is really pointing. Its treasures are the salvation we already have through grace and the promise of its glorious fulfillment when the Lord comes again. Those spiritual treasures represent the days and the years and the sweat and the blood of Jesus in building the house of our faith. Neither Satan nor sin, neither false values nor spiritual laziness, should be allowed to rubble our spiritual house and leave it unprepared for the coming of the Lord, and for eternal glory with him.

Today is the first Sunday of the new liturgical year. It is appropriate that the Church should fill the liturgy with scriptures of the Lord's second coming, and of the promise of our future glory with him. They remind us of our Christian priorities at the start of a new Church year. We are forewarned of the suddenness of the second coming and the need to be prepared. And we are reminded that, in the second coming, everything that is not of Christ will fade away, but that all who are in Christ face a glorious future with him.

4A Second Sunday of Advent

MATTHEW 3:1–12

Prepare the Way!

John the Baptist is the kind of man most of us would not like to meet—neither in the dark of the night nor in the clear of the day. You get the impression that he would read your soul as clear as crystal, and that he might not hesitate to shout your sins out loud for all your friends to hear! He lays into the Pharisees and the Sadducees, and mows them down in front of everyone. His language is extreme. I excuse him only because I believe the man was utterly committed to God, and transparently spiritual.

He is the kind of man that no one could bring before a congressional investigating committee or an ethics board. You could pin nothing on him, and those who might try would be shown up for the fools they are. Sin and its human excuses have no defense in John's blistering presence. I would have no defense in his blistering presence.

John is a herald. He is preparing the way for Jesus and the kingdom; preparing the people for the kingdom involves, first of all, the call to repentance. John, therefore, baptizes with a baptism of repentance. John is fully in the tradition of the Old Testament prophets with his excuse-less, up-front call to repentance and reform. He demands a change of mind and heart in all who would hope to be worthy of receiving the Lord's kingdom. He demands that the Pharisees and the Sadducees show forth in their lives the evidence of that new mind and heart.

A few years ago a friend of mine suffered a stroke. It rattled him. "I assure you," he said to me, "it focused my mind on what really matters. I took it as a grace from God, a wake-up call to get my priorities right."

Is it easier or harder for us today to have the new mind and heart of the Christian, to hold the right priorities, and to show their fruits in our daily lives? That's a difficult question to answer. On the one hand, we have benefits lacking to previous generations. We are better educated. The companies we work for make us familiar with such things as mission statements, goals, objectives, priorities, strategies of execution, and tabled results. Our working week, however long the hours, is shorter than that of our forebears on the farm. It leaves many of us with huge chunks of free time for bar hopping and partying. In this scenario, it should be easier for us to have the right Christian priorities, and to execute them.

On the other hand, each day is so stressed that our psychic energies are drained by our work, and there is no energy or enthusiasm left for feeding the soul. Therefore, I would not want to pass an easy judgment on whether more or less is expected of us today than was expected of our farming forebears. That's God's call, not mine. But I urge all of us to think about my friend and what his stroke did for the new shape of each of his remaining days. Get your priorities right!

John quotes Isaiah: "Prepare the way of the Lord; make straight his path." The economic success of the Western nations, including our own, has been greatly dependent on straight roads; on interstate highways and freeways that move freight quickly from one location to another. Isaiah's vision of how to "make straight in the wasteland a highway for our God" (see Isaiah 40:3–4) is illustrated in the making of these great roads. "Mountains and hills" had to be "leveled"; "valleys" and depressions had to be "filled in"; and the "rough ways" had to be made smooth. That is how Hitler fashioned his *autobahns* so that he could move his military quickly eastward into Poland and Russia to expand the *Reich*. General Dwight D. Eisenhower, commander of the allied forces in Europe in World War II—taking a page from the Third Reich—came home from the war and as president, expanded the interstate highway system to knit the nation together in the interests of unity and commerce. Isaiah is constructing God's highway; John the Baptist is preparing our Lord's highway. They want a road by which God can travel, easily and effectively, straight into our hearts.

Let us allow their words to challenge us. We are, at one and the same time, preparing for the coming of Jesus at Christmas and for the coming of Christ in glory at the end of time. Let us, therefore, level the mountains and hills that are our sins. Let us fill in the valleys that are our failures and omissions. Let us smooth out the roughness of our incivility toward others in our lives. May we burn the chaff of our false idols, excessive consumerism, hollow sophistication, and wrong priorities. In this way, we will "prepare the straight way of the Lord" into our hearts at Christmas and at life's end.

7A Third Sunday of Advent

MATTHEW 11:2–11

The Greatest and the Graced

John the Baptist has been blazing a trail for Jesus, and now he asks, "Are you 'the one who is to come'? or should we look for another?" Did John develop a doubt about Jesus as the promised Messiah? Did John feel that Jesus was turning out to be a Messiah substantially different from the one he expected? Or was it John's disciples who really doubted? Or is Matthew, through this Gospel, answering the same, persisting doubt among his own fellow Christians some years later? We know from the Gospels that most people wanted a politically powerful Messiah, such as Jesus was not.

In reply, our Lord confidently quotes Isaiah's description of the Messiah and says that the profile is—point for point—being realized in himself. It is proven in his words and actions. "Go and tell John what you hear and see: the blind regain their sight and the lame walk, lepers are cleansed and the deaf hear, and the dead are raised, and the poor have the good news preached to them." These are words that only the true Messiah could speak, and Jesus' actions are the works of the true kingdom of God, a kingdom that is full of God's love and healing and justice and compassion. The crucial line for me in this Gospel passage is the last one, "Amen, I say to you, among those born of women there has been none greater than John the Baptist; yet the least in the kingdom of heaven is greater than he."

Our Lord has just painted John in glorious colors. He is our Lord's Elijah. He is the greatest man born of woman. No one quite like John has ever appeared before in history. And yet the least Christian among us is superior to the Baptist! It sounds a bit overdone, but Jesus is telling the truth. How can that be?

The answer is found in the saying, count your blessings! Let you and I do so now by contrasting our position with that of John the Baptist. We are in the kingdom of God: John only foresaw it. He did not live to enjoy it. He reminds me of all the parents of the past who worked themselves to the bone so that their children could have the education and the lifestyle that was never theirs. It was John's destiny to announce the kingdom: it is our destiny to populate it. None of this has anything to do with personal achievement of course, but with our place in salvation history and the grace and goodness of God to us.

The late Scottish theologian William Barclay asked, "What is it that the Christian has that John could never have?" He answered, "John never saw the Cross." John did not live long enough to experience the full range of Christ as Messiah, nor to have his Old Testament theology reshaped by the gentleness, love, and forgiveness of the kingdom that came with Jesus. He did not live long enough to understand the depth of the love of the God of Jesus, and to see it poured out as agony and tears and sweat and blood and death on a cross—for us. He did not live long enough to see the glory of Christ's Resurrection, and to experience its power for making all things possible in this life and the next.

John, magnificent herald of the Messiah and of the kingdom, did not live to experience the range and depth of Jesus and his kingdom of compassionate justice and love. Such was not his destiny. But it is ours. That is why Jesus could say, "I solemnly assure you, history has not known a man born of woman greater than John the Baptist. Yet the least born into the kingdom of God is greater than he."

10A Fourth Sunday of Advent

MATTHEW 1:18–24

Good News, and It Couldn't Be Better

Most of us complain about the media. The media never bring us good news. The stories are all about greed and crime, terrorism, war and brutality, horrific famines, and the latest threats to world peace. The stories are, at times, gruesome and depressing. They keep us on edge. They sap our energy, and they whittle away at our Christian desire to be positive about the world and to trust our neighbors. The media make us suspicious.

If you live long enough under this negative hammering, you may arrive at the psychological point where any good news at all is suspect, and the best of good news is altogether unbelievable. Is that what has happened to the Christmas story, the ultimate in good news? People are still celebrating Christmas all over the world but many of them hardly know why anymore. The stable has been displaced by the shopping mall. It's all so commercialized that, at this time of the year, you see protesting Christians on the streets with placards that read, "Put *Christ* back into *Christ*mas" and "Jesus is the *reason* for the *season*."

Today's Gospel has the ultimate in good news: "She will give birth to a son, and they shall call him *Emmanuel,* a name which means God is with us." This news is staggering, but some of us appreciate it no deeper than our nostalgic childhood memory of the baby in the crib. We shy away from the full truth: that this is the incarnation of God among us—with adult meaning and adult consequences for our lives.

For tens of millions of people in our Western culture, Christmas is just a break from work with a Christmas bonus thrown in. It is a warm, touchy-feely respite in the wilds of mid-winter. It has less and less to do with the astounding good news that God has entered human history, and entered our personal lives.

The second name given to the infant in the Gospel today is *Jesus*. This is the Greek translation of the Hebrew name *Joshua*. *Joshua* means "God is salvation" or "God will save His people." The angel tells Joseph that Jesus will save his people from their sins. This, too, is astounding good news, but are we capable of appreciating it today? Not if we don't sin anymore! Does anyone sin anymore? If we say that we don't sin, then that explains why Christmas has been robbed of its theological foundation, and why Jesus is anything and everything we want him to be except what his name means—the one who saves his people from their sins.

Biblical history depicts a world longing for the birth of its Savior. The world languishes in expectation through the long night of the centuries. These were centuries of sin: Adam's sin, Cain's sin, community sin, social sin, tribal sin, national sin, wider-world sin, and, of course, personal sin. Even the best among the generations remained persons caught in the web of sin; people walking in darkness, longing for the light. God's own chosen people, even *they*, were likened in the Bible to beasts of burden, weighted down by their sins.

Salvation history is, indeed, the story of sin. And it is also a catalog of the unending run of sacrifices and oblations, of sin-offerings and atonements made by people in the hope of release from all of this sin and from all of this accumulated guilt. And salvation history is also the story of the expectation of the Savior, and of the increasing momentum of this expectation as the time of deliverance drew near.

The sense of sin and the felt need of a Savior are dominant in salvation history; they are dead at the present time. That is why the shopping malls boom and the cash registers buzz at Christmastime while more and more people know less and less about what got all of this commerce going in the first place. Christmas is in crisis in the Western world. It is a Christmas without a Savior in it, because our world feels no need of one. Shall we, too, add to the crisis by denying Jesus the meaning of his name?

Some years ago, the dean of American psychiatry, Karl Menninger, wrote his book, *Whatever Became of Sin?* It is an up-front challenge by a psychiatrist to all who have mislaid their sense of personal sin and their responsibility for naming that sin; a challenge to all who wish to hide their sin behind the language of stress, anxiety, predisposition, prior-scripting, mechanisms, triggers, and transferences of various kinds. Certainly, much of our negative behavior and our pathologies have honest origins and are not sinful in the theological sense. But, on the other hand, much of what we attribute to other causes is simply the result of our own plain selfishness and plain sin.

If Menninger had been a theologian instead of a psychiatrist, he couldn't have made a better case for the existence of genuine sin and guilt in our modern lives. And he couldn't have made a better case for allowing Christmas its true meaning—the birth of Jesus who, as his name translates, came "to save his people from their sins."

Christmas

13ABC The Nativity of the Lord

December 24 / At the Vigil Mass

MATTHEW 1:1–25 (LONGER) OR MATTHEW 1:18–25 (SHORTER)

Joy to the World!

Joy to the world: the Lord is near! On this eve of our dear Savior's birth, I wish you a joyful Christmas!

The Gospel proclamation, which we have just heard, is part of Saint Matthew's introduction to the wonderful story of Christmas. It gives us some wonderful insights into the child that was born on that first Christmas night. It is these insights that allow us to announce joy to the world.

Our Gospel reading highlights three things. The first is the role of the Holy Spirit in the birth of the child of Christmas. The second is the name that Joseph is told to give the child, the name *Jesus*. The third is the name Matthew himself applies to the child, the name *Emmanuel*. These three items form the core of the Christmas event and story.

Theologian William Barclay tells us that, in the theology of the Jewish people, the Holy Spirit of God had certain definite functions. Chief among these was the Spirit's role in bringing God's truth to the people. It was the Spirit of God that inspired the prophets of old. "It was the Holy Spirit who taught the prophets what to say" *(Daily Study Bible: Matthew)*. Now, in today's Gospel, the Holy Spirit's role is not to speak another word of God through another prophet but, marvelously, to allow the entire word of God to be conceived and born of the Virgin Mary. Just as the earth was created through the Word of God, now it will be re-created by the Word made man.

The name that the angel tells Joseph to give the child is *Jesus*. What does *Jesus* mean? It is a form of the name *Joshua*. It means "he shall save [his people] from sin." Names often signified vocations or the special work a person was called upon to do. Jesus' calling is to save from sin—to be the Savior. It is sin that puts distance between us and God. The child of Christmas will save us from our sins and from the distance they put between ourselves and God.

Once the distance is removed God is able to come close to us, even to be with us. And so, Matthew gives the child to be born a name associated in the Old Testament with the majestic God enthroned. It is the name *Emmanuel*—and it means "God-with-us." The scholar John P. Meier writes: "It is precisely by removing sin from his people that Jesus removes the accursed distance and makes God present among his people" *(New Testament Message: Matthew)*.

For you and I to celebrate a Christmas that means more than just its tinsel and its trappings, we need to appreciate these insights that Matthew offers of the child of Christmas. Through Mary's child, the Holy Spirit will restore and renew the face of the earth. Because of Mary's child, God's people will be saved from their sins, and the distance between them and their God, removed. In Mary's child, God will be born in time, among us, and in our personal life stories. "In the beginning was the Word, and the Word was with God, and the Word was God. . . . And the Word became flesh and made his dwelling among us" (John 1:1, 14). These are the reasons why Christmas is truly joy to the world, and joy in our own hearts.

14ABC The Nativity of the Lord

December 25 / Mass at Midnight

LUKE 2:1–14

For Unto Us a Child Is Born

Christmas may be a pure and simple story, but it is also multi-faceted. I mean that it is so full of meaning that the Church requires a whole octave of scripture readings to cover this feast, and to attempt to exhaust its wonder and beauty.

What I share with you now is more a meditation and a memory than a homily. I do so because I feel that each of us approaches Christmas in a very personal way. I believe that, however we approach this feast, Christmas Past—the Christmas of our childhood—has a huge influence on us. Past Christmases have shaped our present personalities and our faith. They have shaped yours and they have shaped mine.

At this time of year, memories flood my heart with moments of childhood awe before crib and carolers; before Christmas lights in windows and almonded, frosted cakes; sitting with family and friends in front of the fireplace, and green and red crepe paper bells multiplying in the mirror above it; before tinsel and garlands rising and falling, as if by magic, on the secret thermals of the room; before the intoxication of shining stars sequining the frosty ground at our feet as we made our early morning way to Mass to welcome the newborn Lord.

There, in that town of my childhood, among the warmest hearts in the world, Bethlehem happened every year. It just had to, for here were men and women to match the best of the sons and daughters of Israel. A Child was born to us; a Son was given us. He was my parents' Son and my Brother. His name was "Wonderful," "Counselor," "Mighty God," and "Prince of Peace."

He was everything the priests and teachers said he was—
the Chosen one, the Desire of all the Ages, the Messiah, the Savior,
the Lord. We knew it, we believed it, and we loved him for it. How we
loved him! I always wondered why he was not first born in my town
rather than in far-off Bethlehem of Judah. There were no overcrowded
inns in my town, no darkened windows, and no closed doors. There
were just close families and humble homes full of stability, security,
and love. He should have been born first in my town. I knew it. We all
knew it. But, seemingly, his Father did not!

It is all so long ago. But it may as well be yesterday, so fresh
and so vibrant the memory. Each Christmas, I put aside the baggage
of a lifetime—the studies and the theologies, the titles and the roles,
the good and the bad of the journey of my life—to kneel my heart
before this many-splendored Infant in his manger of my memory.
I whisper my surest theology to him, the little things said long ago when
I was not much older than he and all the worthwhile world was found
within my lovely town.

Lord, little one and mighty one: be born in the Bethlehem of every
town of the earth that has faith in you, in the Bethlehem of every home that
has love for you, in the Bethlehem of every heart that hopes for you. Above
all, be born this day with your healing and peace in the houses of hearts
divided by sin, beset by anxiety, broken by disappointment, and haunted by
loss and loneliness. Christmas only heightens their pain. Be born among these.
They are truly the poverty-stricken of the earth on this day of days.

15ABC The Nativity of the Lord

December 25 / Mass at Dawn

LUKE 2:15–20

Our Winter's Light

I wish you, dear regular parishioners, a merry and blessed Christmas. I wish you, our visitors home for Christmas, a merry and blessed Christmas. I wish you among us today who may be distanced from the Church for whatever reason, a merry and blessed Christmas. We are all God's family, and He is delighted that all of us are worshipping here together on this blessed day of His Son's birth. All of us belong at the manger—no exceptions.

Much of the story of Christmas is a story of light in darkness. Christ is born in the night. He is born in the dark of winter. But a bright star appears in the dark sky. And the angels light up the night sky with the glory of God that surrounds them as they sing their hosannas. And most important of all, the world that has been chained in the long night of sin and error receives its awaited liberation of light. The prophet Isaiah promised it 700 years in advance: "The people who walked in darkness have seen a great light; upon those who dwelt in the land of gloom a light has shone" (Isaiah 9:1). The infant in the manger is that promised light.

When I wish you a merry Christmas, what does that mean? The Russian novelist Fyodor Dostoyevsky wrote, "While we are on earth, we grope . . . as though in the dark. . . . But for the precious image of Christ before us, we would lose our way . . ." (Memoirs). Cardinal Newman wrote, "Lead, kindly light, amid the encircling gloom, lead Thou me on; the night is dark, and I am far from home, lead Thou me on" (Lead, Kindly Light).

Many of us today are a bit lost in a sort of dark, experiencing a sort of encircling gloom. We are not always able to name it. It's a feeling, a sense we have, dissatisfaction within. It may be the gloom of disillusioned love, the dark of sin, the night of addiction, the dark of depression, the winter of pain and loss, the gloom of short-term contracts and repossessed cars, the dark of inquiries and audits. Many of us are working our fingers to the bone in the competitive economy and still wonder what it's all about. We get some release through our wild weekends, our trips to Las Vegas or New York, and the NFL on wide-screen, surround-sound TV. But after a year, or two, or three of this we feel like, "Is that all there is to life"—a sort of gloom, a sort of fog, a sort of dark, a sort of night?

Christmas says, "That's not all there is to it!" Christmas says, "You need something more, and there is something more!" Christmas says, "The people who walk in darkness have seen a great light!" The Welsh poet Dylan Thomas says, "Light breaks where no sun shines" *(Light Breaks where No Sun Shines)*. John Newman says, "Lead, kindly light!" Dostoyevsky says, "We grope as though in the dark. . . . But for the precious image of Christ before us, we would lose our way."

Today, Christ is born among us and for us. Accept him into your heart. Walk through life with him at your side. He will put light and meaning on everything that crosses your path. And he will love and cherish you every step of the way. To wish you a merry Christmas is to wish that Christ be born not just in Bethlehem of Judea but in the Bethlehem of your heart; not just in the winter straw of a poor manger far away but in the warm love of your responding heart. And I do wish you that merry Christmas!

16ABC The Nativity of the Lord

December 25 / Mass during the Day

JOHN 1:1–18 (LONGER) OR JOHN 1:1–5, 9–14 (SHORTER)

The Mystery of God's Love

I wish you, dear people, a blessed Christmas. May it mean the birth of Jesus in the stable of your heart with all his healing and comfort and love for you and for those you hold dear.

Some of us here this morning are not regular churchgoers; some of us are. Even among the regulars there are, most likely, many shades of faith. That may be because our faith has been bruised a bit by a failed marriage, or by our children's fall from faith despite our prayers, or by the scandal of religious hate and terrorism, or by the growing secularization of society which whittles away at our spiritual core. Those of us who are not regular churchgoers may be so for no greater reason than that we've lost the habit of it somewhere along the road of life. In all of our cases, the heart has its reasons for whatever deep or shallow faith we swim in, and I am no one's judge. Rather, I'd like to be your support in some small way.

All of us came here to church this morning despite our varying degrees of faith. This means that Christmas is still important to us, whatever our motives are for being here. We may wonder if we're really here just to please the spouse, or the kids, or to keep tongues from wagging, or because of custom, sentiment, nostalgia, and the ghost of a dearly loved grandma. Perhaps it doesn't matter all that much. Perhaps any one of these less-than-perfect motives is, nonetheless, the grace that God uses to draw us here in worship so that He may touch us once more with His love.

You may have read items telling you that Christmas is just the Christian makeover of an old pagan feast. You may wonder if it's just the echo of an earlier human form of winter celebration. You may wonder if Christmas is largely based on the gathering long ago of the family, the tribe, around a roaring fire to affirm life at the lowest time of the year and to shake a collective fist in the face of the frosty god of winter.

John, in today's Gospel, says that Christmas is much more. He says it's the celebration of the mystery of God's love for you and for me. Christmas means that God's love took human form in the baby born in the stable in Bethlehem. In this way, God made His invisible love for us visible, His intangible heart tangible.

John speaks of Christmas with the hindsight of the years he spent in the company of the Christmas child that grew up and became Jesus of Nazareth. It is John's experience of Jesus of Nazareth that allows him to tell us that the Christmas baby is more than a helpless babe in the straw. The baby is the beginning human form of the Word of God full of grace and truth. The life and ministry of the adult Jesus proved it for John. Jesus turned out to be the forgiveness of God for us poor sinners and God's warmth and love and light in the darkness of our winter world.

Jesus turned out to be the power by which John—and you and I—are able to answer the age-old questions that trouble our friends and contemporaries and maybe even ourselves at times: What's it all about? Why am I here? What might give deeper meaning and purpose to my life? Who can guarantee me a future beyond the grave that seems to end everything?

John found his answers in the baby of Bethlehem who became Jesus of Nazareth. We and our questioning friends can too. In Jesus we are able to live lives of purpose and fulfillment and inner joy. Jesus is the pattern and the power of what each one of us is called to be and can be: a graced human being, a child of God, a person with purpose, someone with a future.

We *are* worthwhile. Christmas means that we are *very* worthwhile in God's eyes. For all our bruises and our failures and our sins, and whether we are regulars or irregulars in our faith and at Sunday worship, we are called by God and we are the beloved of God. You and I, dear friends, are worth the Christmas that God's love makes possible for us. That is what the infant in the manger is telling each one of us this blessed Christmas Day.

17A The Holy Family of Jesus, Mary, and Joseph

Sunday within the Octave of Christmas

Matthew 2:13−15, 19−23

God's Family

We find ourselves on the pages of the scriptures. We find those who people our lives on the same pages with us. We find in the scriptures the same challenges and opportunities for us that faced prior Christian generations. We find the options we may choose from. And we find the grace of God pushing us toward the best decisions.

I look at this Holy Family in the Gospel and marvel at its unquestioning faith and love. There is no word of doubt from Mary. There is no word of frustration from Joseph. There is no record of any word of any kind from either of them. God (through the angel) does the talking: the little family obeys without question. It is a lesson for us not about slavish obedience but about absolute trust in God.

The Holy Family is in exile in Egypt because of Herod. He seeks the life of the child Jesus. In the history of the Hebrew people, Egypt is the traditional land of exile, the place of flight in time of persecution, and the place of refuge in time of famine.

The little family cannot go home. It lives under threat and stress. There is the price of blood on the head of the child. Our families fall apart under much, much less. What held the Holy Family together? Surely it was the intense respect and love of the family members among themselves and their unquestioning reliance on the goodness and the grace of God. Is there not the model here for holding our own families together under stress? If mutual respect and trust in God are maintained, then love need not be shattered.

This short homily can only touch on two or three aspects of family life. The first is this: The family today, as the Holy Family back then, has to deal with stress and threat. It will hold itself together and even grow in solidarity and grace if respect and love characterize its members and if they put genuine trust in God. This is not just "pious talk"! God is not someone unrelated to family life, to its joys and sorrows, its stresses and strains. God in Christ (to use Saint Paul's expression) was the child in the refugee family in Egypt and he was the child in the later settled family of Nazareth. Turn to him, then, in family difficulties for understanding and support.

Secondly, the *Catechism of the Catholic Church* calls the Christian family "a domestic church." It is "in itself a realization of ecclesial communion, . . . community of faith, hope and charity" (#2204). This Christian family, your family, may be looked upon as the Church in miniature. Each Christian family is a kind of microcosm of the wider parish and diocese. This parish could style itself as "A Family of Families." I think that this is a most relevant description because our Christian families are the flesh and blood of our parishes. The vitality of the parish depends greatly on them. Its faith depends greatly on them and the passing on of the faith. Its love depends greatly on them and the spread of charity throughout the parish community. Its hope of the future depends greatly on them. Its hope of the future is its membership of tomorrow and the priestly vocations to serve that membership of tomorrow.

Thirdly, the Christian family, your family, is also an institution in the front line and on the firing line of social life and social problems. On the one hand, it is pressured on many sides and often questioned and criticized. On the other hand, great expectations are vested in it and a healthful, compassionate neighborhood, society, and nation depend on it. We pray for all Christian families today, and especially for those of our own parish. May the Holy Family support them each day in their endeavors and their hopes. May the Holy Family unite them in peace and in love.

18ABC The Blessed Virgin Mary, Mother of God

January 1/The Octave Day of Christmas

LUKE 2:16–21

A New Year's Wish

The "things" that Mary treasured are found in the story that the shepherds told. The most important "thing" is the centerpiece of the story—her baby is the long-awaited Savior. His name is Jesus-Savior, and under that name he is circumcised, that is, dedicated to God for God's work on earth.

But Mary is surely treasuring other "things" as well, other related "things." She cannot but reflect on and treasure the meaning of the Christmas event in her own regard. She cannot but marvel at her God-giftedness and gracefulness in being chosen as the mother of the world's Savior. We are told that this was the dream of every girl throughout the Jewish generations. The Second Vatican Council says, "After a long period of waiting the times are fulfilled in her, the exalted Daughter of Sion, and the new plan of salvation is established" (*Lumen gentium*, 55).

Mary is, as the Council says of her, one of the redeemed as all of us are. But she is redeemed "in a more exalted fashion" than we (*Lumen gentium*, 53). Her redemption is more exalted because we are born tainted with sin, but not she. "From the first moment of her conception . . . and by virtue of the [future] merits of Jesus Christ . . . she was preserved immune from all stain of original sin" (Pius IX, *Ineffabilis Deus*). Mary is the recipient of other graces and privileges. She is their recipient because of her unique personal holiness, and because of her unique calling in life, and because of the manner in which she did everything in obedience to God's word.

In what scripture calls the fullness of time, Mary conceived and gave birth to "him in whom dwells the whole fullness of deity bodily" (Colossians 2:9). The one in whom the fullness of deity dwells is, of course, Jesus. He is God become man and he is Mary's child. He is, as the *Catechism of the Catholic Church* puts it, "the One whom she conceived as man by the Holy Spirit, who truly became her Son according to the flesh, [and] was none other than the Father's eternal Son, the second person of the Holy Trinity." Hence, the Church is able to confess Mary as the "Mother of God" (CCC, 466).

It is under that title, Mother of God, that we honor Mary in today's feast. It is a title that is both integral to the Christmas story and a consequence of it. It is the reality that was included, however veiled to them, in the glad tidings of the angels and in the marvelous report given by the shepherds. And it surely is one of the "things" Mary reflected on and treasured in her heart. We, too, should treasure her title of Mother of God because, as Abbot Anscar Vonier, OSB, rightly noted, it is not a passing title, passing into nothingness once the Word is born in time. Mary is "permanently the Mother of God. Hers is an abiding dignity" *(The Divine Motherhood)*.

When we pray to Mary we are, therefore, praying to the Mother of God. Under that title and through its reality she has immense intercessory power with God on our behalf. And since she is not only the Lord's mother but the mother of the Church and our spiritual mother as well, we may turn to her with utmost confidence knowing that she has a mother's heart in all matters relating to our well-being. "Pray for us, O Holy Mother of God, that we may be made worthy of the promises of Christ."

My New Year's wish is that we, as individuals and as Church, will continue to honor Mary as the Mother of God and our mother too, and that we may be full of confidence when turning to her in our need. Not a single one of our needs is deeper than the reach of our mother's love and the power of her intercession.

19ABC Second Sunday after Christmas

JOHN 1:1–18 (LONGER) OR JOHN 1:1-5, 9–14 (SHORTER)

Crib and Cosmos

Since Christmas, the Liturgy of the Word has been busy trying to give us as full a picture as it can of Jesus. Each day since Christmas the Gospel readings draw out for us the range of meaning that can be found in the child that was born on Christmas Day.

So . . . we've had Gospel readings about the infant in the manger who is a helpless babe in the straw. We learn from this that God makes Himself utterly vulnerable and commits Himself to our trust. The angel tells us that the infant is also, in fact, the long-awaited Savior of God's people. We are challenged to resurrect our sense of sin. Then we meet this babe as the remarkable child in the temple, discussing the Law with the learned rabbis and asking insightful questions. Today, through the soaring theological mind of John, we meet the infant as the cosmic Christ. For he, too, was born on that first Christmas Day.

John writes for people of a Hellenistic background. They are people with a philosophical frame of mind. John does not wish to present Jesus to them through a Jewish theology. They would be lost in its Jewish categories. He goes straight to the philosophy they understand. They are a people who admire the *logos:* the word or the mind of God that creates the orderliness and the beauty of the world. And so, he pens this wonderful prologue: "In the beginning was the *logos*-Word . . . the *logos*-Word was with God . . . all things were created through the *logos*-Word . . . and that *logos*-Word became flesh and lived among us." Now, let me tell you his whole story! Let me uncover for you this Word and Wisdom that you so admire! It is a person. It is the Son of God. His name is Jesus of Nazareth.

Our own generation is characterized by its concern for the human and the personal. What does being human mean? What does personhood entail? How does one achieve true humanity? The whole world has an opinion on these questions and, perhaps, we are confused by the plethora of opinions.

Talk shows offer definitions of the human and the personal. So do celebrities. So does every homespun philosopher with a soapbox to stand on. Psychology and philosophy offer critically thought-out descriptions. So does John Paul II. He never stops. Apart altogether from his position as pope, he is a considerable philosopher on this issue of humanness and personhood. No wonder young people flock to him. They are looking for their self-identity. He's always at work defining for them who they are. According to John Paul II, one becomes truly human by living the pattern that God set in the humanity of Jesus, and one reaches the highest level of personhood when one's human potential reaches its full maturity through grace. That can only happen "in Christ." Saint Paul says the same thing. So does Saint John.

Was it Macbeth who said that life is "but a walking shadow"? Was it Sartre who said that a human being is just "a useless passion"? Was it Yeats who wished to "unriddle the universe"? Today's Gospel says that the Word of God, the cosmic Christ, is the one that unriddles the universe and the one that defines the human person as no science or technology ever will. It is not their job to try. So what are we doing? Are we putting Christ forward to our anxious world as the pattern of personhood? Are we telling our confused youth and our semi-agnostic fellow workers that life can be just as questionable and as stupid for us as it is for them, but that, in Christ, we have a handle on the mystery? Are we telling suicidal young students that Jesus is the key to treasures of comfort and support deeper than any stress and more satisfying than any TV commercial claiming to offer them intense taste, gusto, life, and whatever?

So many others—gunmen, thugs, bullies, and addicts—are loose on our mean modern streets because they are adrift of Christ and have lost the sense of what is human and precious in their victims and in themselves. All that can be changed in Christ!

Are we ourselves content to stay with our childish version of Christianity, the version that fails us—and fails the teens we model for—in the ambushes of life? Do we not wish to grow into adult faith, and experience the depth of God's love now in this life that John and the others came to know so intimately?

Snapshot homilies and prayers in the gap will not cut the mustard anymore for the homilist or for the adult believer located in a questioning age. All of us need to prioritize Jesus the Word in our everyday agenda, and we need a seriously reflective engagement with the Gospels about that Word so that we may know what it is to be human, and how one achieves optimum personhood. Only then will we have an adult grip on this "Word became flesh and made his dwelling among us." Only then will we have a fitting adult religious experience that parallels John's. We ought to be able to say what he was able to say of himself and of the other disciples: "Of Christ's fullness we have all had a share—love following upon love."

20ABC The Epiphany of the Lord

January 6

MATTHEW 2:1–12

The Meaning of the Magi

Epiphany means the showing forth. The baby born in Bethlehem is presented, in this lovely story of the magi (or wise men or kings or astrologers), as the Savior of all the nations and not just of his own people, Israel. Just as there is equal opportunity and equal rights these days, so in the Savior is there equal opportunity of salvation for all of God's children.

The point of the story, then, is to have the magi, as the representatives of all the nations, present at the birth of the world's Savior. In them, our Gentile forebears, you and I—of all races and of all colors—were present when Christ was born. Before that moment, we were religious outsiders to God and to grace. But through the magi we were chosen for intimacy with the Lord.

The gifts that the magi placed at the foot of the manger were gold, frankincense, and myrrh. Gold symbolizes royalty, incense symbolizes divinity. Early Christian tradition understood these gifts as signaling the kingship and the divinity of Jesus. Myrrh was seen as a prophecy about the child's future death, since myrrh is a resin that was used in perfume and in the anointing of the body for burial. We may interpret the magi's gifts in that manner.

Another interpretation is possible. Magi appear elsewhere in the New Testament scriptures as magicians, or practitioners of the black arts. Examples are Simon Magus and Elymas the magician. In this interpretation, the magi were magicians—outsiders to the world of orthodox religion—who gave up the instruments of their shady trade when they met the Infant. Incense/smoke hid the magician's subterfuge, and myrrh/resin/adhesive gum made objects marvelously disappear (stuck to your arm under your sleeve!). Gold stands for the ill-gotten profit of their art. They surrendered it all as their darkness gave way to the light of Christ. All fraudulent claims, and all false values, must surrender to the light of Christ.

Either interpretation is rich in meaning for us. It's time for us to make our own journey of faith to the Infant, following his star and not our own. It's time to surrender the darkness of our false values to the light of his true values. It's time to place at his feet the instruments of our black arts that are the works of darkness we do against good conscience, God, and neighbor.

It's time for us to offer the Savior our most prized gold, which is our heart; the incense that is genuine prayer from the heart; and the myrrh that is our works of love for others. It's time for us older Christians especially—after so many Christmases—to be wise men and women who walk with commitment in the light of Christ, and whose hearts are always pining for their place at the manger of their salvation.

21A The Baptism of the Lord

Sunday after January 6
First Sunday in Ordinary Time

MATTHEW 3:13–17

A Statement about Service

Jesus did not need a baptism of repentance, nor one of conversion
in any form. This is indicated by the surprise of John the Baptist when
Jesus presented himself to John for baptism. On the other hand, Jesus
says to John that the baptismal ritual is necessary for him in order
to fulfill God's will. What does he mean?

Our Lord does not masquerade through rituals. So, how
are we to understand this baptism of his? Some scholars suggest that
our Lord submitted to John's baptism as an act of solidarity with
his fellow Jews who were flocking to John. John the Baptist had stirred
the hearts of his countrymen to repentance, and Jesus wished to
encourage that repentance among them. It was also the appropriate
moment for Jesus to launch his own mission—with the trail already
blazed for him by the herald John—and he launched that mission
with a symbolic baptism.

I look to the other readings today in order to see how the
Church understands Jesus' baptism. The first reading—Isaiah—is
especially indicative. Isaiah gives us a profile of the Servant of Yahweh-
God. Jesus is the servant of God, the "man for others" in German
theologian Dietrich Bonhoeffer's words. The servant of God is one who
places distance between himself and the aggressive lords of the earth.
He will have nothing to do with violence, with conquest, with justice based on an eye for an eye and a tooth for a tooth. His person, his
kingdom, and his followers will state the case—and with their lives—
for service expressed as love and mercy. I read the Lord's baptism,
therefore, as his consecration by the Father as the messianic servant.
I also read it as his own personal statement in public of the ministry
of service he was embarking upon with full acceptance and with

lasting commitment. In other words, the Lord's baptism is a ritual statement about service. So, in parallel, must be our own.

Every African missionary has heard of the legendary Albert Schweitzer. He's the genius who, a few generations ago, left his place at the pinnacle of European scholarship to build his medical compound for lepers on the bank of a river in Africa. There he practiced his singular Christian insight: respect for life at all its levels and in all its forms. No exceptions.

Schweitzer wished on us the blessing of finding the secret of a happy life. He said it is service to others. He hoped we would make the discovery early in our lives, lest we make it only at the door of death, with wistful regret.

Jesus is the servant of God and the servant of others. We, too, are in solidarity with him.

The ingredients of our Christian ministry of service are clear. They are found in the Old Testament messianic texts. They are encapsulated in the servant songs of the prophet Isaiah. They are personified in the actions of Jesus. They are popularized in the old catechism lists of the spiritual and corporal works of mercy that we learned as children in school. We are strong on the corporal works today, such as feeding the hungry, clothing the naked, and visiting people who are ill and in prison. But, then, so is even the secular world for all its agnosticism.

But we are surely weak on the spiritual (i.e. catechetical) works, whether we name these the re-evangelization of our country or ongoing Christian formation in our parishes and in our families. Using the old words of the spiritual works of mercy, we may ask ourselves, are we instructing the ignorance of adult faith that is so widespread in our time? Are we counseling and encouraging and challenging, as needs be, those among us with doubts of faith and experiences of abuse, addiction, and moral difficulty of various kinds? Are we pulling our weight for Christ and for his kingdom in the modern marketplace of ideas and lifestyles where others, with so much less to offer, are confidently active? It's our call.

There is no reason why we should fail to see our own Baptism in Christ, like his in the Jordan, as our statement of service to others, for the sake of the kingdom of God.

Lent

22A First Sunday of Lent

MATTHEW 4:1–11

Being Tested

The readings for our liturgy today are a study in contrasts. The main one is between Adam who is deceived and Jesus, the new Adam, who chases the deceiver from his presence. The human side of us is easily taken in: the Christian side of us should not be.

The temptation of Jesus, as it is commonly called, is really a *testing* of his faith in God, a testing of his personal integrity, and a testing of his suitability for his mission. In surviving the test, wholeheartedly and unquestioningly, he is all the more ready for his saving mission.

It is commonplace for you and me to talk about temptation or testing in terms of our human weaknesses. Satan is said to strike us through our weaknesses. We are very weak, scripture says, in the flesh and before the lure of this world. Greed, power, money, and fame attract us. So do pleasure and sloth. But for some of us, perhaps, the lure of the world may be more a matter of its beauty, of our loving its energy too much, of being too at home in the world, of feeling no rush to leave it and to move beyond the naturally sacramental to the purely spiritual. Maybe it's the temptation to remain in some sense forever earthbound. The ultimate letting go may be the hardest loss of all.

If scripture attests that we are tempted through our weaknesses, recent social history on both sides of the Atlantic attests that we are tempted through our privileges. The public record, with which we are all familiar, is sobering—the sins and shenanigans allowed by diplomatic immunity, government privilege, corporate deals, insider trading, cooked books, golden circles, and various elite clubs and castes. So many of our whitest-collared citizens have come to grief through their privileged positions. Some among the privileged in the Church have been scuttled too.

We are also tempted through our talents. Some of us come to grief through our talents. Talents so easily allow us to rise above others; to know-it-all, be-it-all, or pretend-it-all. On the contrary, talents

are like wealth. They are a great moral responsibility; given us in trust
for the people those talents are intended to serve. Jesus said, "Much
will be required of the person entrusted with much, and still more will
be demanded of the person entrusted with more" (Luke 12:48).

Our Lord was tested intensely in today's Gospel. We may
be tested only mildly by comparison, but we are tested every day and
through the course of each day. We may have no dramatic confrontation with Satan such as Jesus had. But there is the testing of our
personal integrity, and the testing of our weaknesses, and the testing
of our talents. And there is that other thing—the "petty pace," in
Shakespeare's words *(Macbeth,* V), of each day, and of every day's
recurring aggravations. It is enough for us to handle these well. With
God's grace, we recommit ourselves today to the test.

25A Second Sunday of Lent

MATTHEW 17:1–9

My Three Faces

The incident in the Gospel today is the transfiguration of Jesus on
the mountain—traditionally Tabor, probably Hermon. We are much
deeper into Matthew's Gospel today than we've been for the past
few Sundays. We are, correspondingly, much deeper into the ministry
of Jesus. In fact, he's about to go to Jerusalem—and Calvary.

Before him lies his approaching death. As he so often does,
our Lord goes up the mountain to pray to his Father before this
critical event in his life. Perhaps he wants to ask his Father to strengthen
him for the journey to Calvary. When the Transfiguration is over, the
Lord is steeled in heart and spirit to sacrifice his life for us.

His apostles, too, need to know something. They need some
better insight into the meaning of Jesus as the Messiah. They, too,
need assurance that the scandal they will soon find in the cross is not
the end; that it is necessary; and that all will end in glory for their
Lord and for themselves.

And so, the Lord is transfigured with glory on the mountain. His face dazzles as the sun and his clothes become as radiant as light. Moses' face once shone on Mount Sinai with the reflected glory of God (see Exodus 34:29). The apostles see a new Jesus on the mountain. It is a preview, as it were, of his future glory beyond the cross.

Moses and Elijah are present. They represent the Law and the Prophets. They are in conversation with Jesus. What are they saying? Perhaps they are offering him reassurances as to his cross and—through it—his crown. Peter is so mesmerized by the whole scene that he wants to set up three booths or tents. He recalled, perhaps, how the Israelites once lived in tents in the wilderness, and that they would live again in tents—so it was believed by the Jews—in the messianic age.

A bright cloud overshadows them. It is the *shechinah*, the luminous cloud that covered the Israelites during the Exodus, the cloud that signaled the presence of the glory of God. A voice speaks out of the cloud confirming Jesus as God's beloved Son. Our Lord is strengthened and confirmed as to his unique sonship, his necessary cross, and his glorious future beyond it, and because of it. The lesson for us can hardly be different. Carrying our daily cross, in imitation of Jesus, is our own prelude to glory.

There is a second lesson we can draw from this event. Just as Jesus had his Transfiguration and the apostles saw him in a different light than they were used to, so too we have our transfigurations. I'll illustrate this with reference to a story that Francois Mauriac of the French Academy once wrote. The story is an imaginary interview with the legendary Greta Garbo. She was considered so hauntingly beautiful by men of the silent screen era that they called her simply "the Face."

In the interview, Garbo tells Mauriac why she no longer appears in movies or in public, and why she hides as a recluse all the time. She has three faces, she says. There is the baby face she was born with. There is the adult face that is now beginning to wrinkle with age. And there is the celluloid face in the movies that has been transfigured in the adoring imaginations of millions of men and women. It is that transfigured face that she wants all men and women to remember. And so she hides her aging face.

There is no need for us to hide who are in Christ. Our transfigurations follow the right order, and we are happy to show our three faces to everyone. Our three faces are the Christian face we were given at our Baptism, the maturing Christian face we have now as grace transforms it more and more each day, and the final face we will wear, the one transfigured in dazzling glory, when the good Lord comes again.

28A Third Sunday of Lent

John 4:5–42 (longer) or
John 4:5–15, 19b–26, 39a, 40–42 (shorter)

The Water of Life

The Bible has many theologies. One of them is the theology of water. (There is a parallel theology of bread.)

In the very first line of Genesis, water is already present. It is the primeval water of the earth's formation. God divides it into the rain of the sky and the water of the ocean. Then He divides the water of the ocean until it allows dry land to appear. Forms of life begin to teem on the dry land, but they will always depend on the waters of the sky for their existence. Without water, life is not possible. This is a basic of the Jewish experience.

Water was critical to the Jews of old. They lived not just on dry land but in desert land. They lived or died by the flow of water. Everything depended on it: their crops, their flocks, their very selves. Water was their dearest commodity, their indispensable resource, and the grace of God in their midst. When the rain fell and the water flowed, they knew that God was with them. When it ceased to flow, they worried and wondered where He had gone.

Water was so crucial to their existence that they made it into a primary religious symbol. It came to stand for the grace of God that revived their souls: "The Lord is my shepherd; I shall not want. In verdant pastures he gives me repose; by restful waters he leads me; he refreshes my soul" (Psalm 23:1–2). Water also came to stand for the continuing presence of God with His people. It pre-dated and post-dated the cloud by day and the pillar of fire by night that signaled

God's presence during the Exodus. "Can God spread a table for us in the desert?" the Israelites asked. "Yes, they spoke against God, saying, 'Can God spread a table in the desert? For when he struck the rock, waters gushed forth, and the streams overflowed. Can he also give bread and provide meat for his people?'" (Psalm 78:19–20). For the Jews, the *continuing* presence of God in water is unlike his once-off presence in the cloud and in the fire.

Jesus now enters this Jewish theology of water and expands it. ". . . whoever drinks of the water I shall give will never thirst," he says to the woman at the well. "The water I shall give will welcome in him a spring of water welling up to eternal life." "Sir, give me this water," she says. The water Jesus speaks of is his word and his grace. It pours into our hearts in scripture and sacrament, and it wells us up into eternal life.

We are so blessed! We come into history under what is called the Christian dispensation. God is present to us, not in symbol of cloud and fire and Jewish water, but in his Son's all-powerful word and grace. We hear that word every time we are present at the liturgy: "The word of the Lord . . . The gospel of the Lord." We experience His presence in His Word as a presence of caring for us, sentence after sentence, of comforting us in our losses, of encouraging us in our successes and in our weaknesses, of urging us on, with hope in our hearts, to the glory that awaits us.

And we experience God's presence in the calm of the moments after Holy Communion when the *anam chara*, the soul-friend Spirit, whispers his assurance that Jesus is now in our hearts as the Lover of each of us that no poor human in our lives, no matter how good, can compete with. And we are given the pledge that what Jesus promised us remains as enduring and as satisfying as the day he first spoke it: "Whoever eats my flesh and drinks my blood has eternal life, and I will raise him on the last day" (John 6:54). All of this Jesus had in mind when he said to the woman, "I can give you water welling up into eternal life."

31A Fourth Sunday of Lent

JOHN 9:1–41 (LONGER) OR
JOHN 9:1, 6–9, 13–17, 34–38 (SHORTER)

Living the Light We Are

I believe you all know what the "chunnel" is. It is a tunnel dug under-neath the English channel between England and France. One of the remarkable features of the chunnel, as the British call it, is the accuracy of its engineering. Two massive boring machines started on either side of the English Channel and met in the middle. The chunnel is, in fact, three tunnels—one for rail freight, one for passenger rail, and a service tunnel in between.

The pool of Siloam, in today's Gospel story, is also quite an engineering feat for its time. The chunnel goes through chalk; the tunnel that created the pool of Siloam goes through rock. It carried Jerusalem's water supply from the Kidron valley. God, through the engineers, "sent" the water from Kidron to Siloam—hence, the pool's name Siloam, which means "sent."

Our Lord uses this incident of the man born blind to illustrate a tragedy far greater than physical blindness—spiritual blindness. The man born blind cannot see. It's not his fault or his parents' fault. Physical blindness was common among our Lord's contemporaries, and for many reasons, including the lack of hygiene and a harsh, glaring climate. Our Lord is particularly grieved by the opposition of the Pharisees and their spiritual blindness in refusing to accept him as the Messiah. They knew better. They were educated in the Law and the Prophets. They knew what the Messiah should look like. And they saw the Messiah's profile in Jesus. But they rejected him. Indeed, the great tragedy of the age of Jesus was that so many, who were physically sighted, were spiritually unsighted when it came to recog-nizing him as the Messiah.

If we just think about it for a few moments we come to realize how prevalent and how unnecessary spiritual blindness is in our own time too. To begin with, few of us are not physically blind in this age of medical technology, nor need we live in spiritual darkness in the age of universal education. None of us need to suffer the blindness of religious ignorance, bigotry, hatred, inhumanity, incivility, and ignorance of the hell of drugs, ignorance of moral values, and the lack of spiritual direction.

None of us is out there in the Palestine of two thousand years ago, in a blinding sun, farming from pre-dawn to darkness, and too exhausted to talk to God at the end of the day. None of us is so educationally marginalized that we cannot read a magazine or a TV guide or the football schedule of our favorite team—or a line of scripture or a prayer card. None of us, in the age of civil rights and social sensitivity, need rush blindly to judge others by their appearance only; nor need we, in the age of media revelations and exposés, walk ourselves blindly toward some future day of reckoning with the traffic court, or the tax auditors, or with our long-suffering spouse and children.

And none of us, in this generation, need go before God at the end and say, "I didn't know," "I couldn't read," "No one ever told me," "I was forced to live in darkness," or "I was too blind to see." The price of our modern education and of our easy access to knowledge of all kinds, including knowledge of the Lord and his way, is increased personal responsibility.

34A Fifth Sunday of Lent

JOHN 11:1–45 (LONGER) OR
JOHN 11:3–7, 17, 20–27, 33B–45 (SHORTER)

Reading This Map Called Life

All of us hear this Gospel when we attend funerals. It is not just an affirmation of life but an affirmation of life beyond the earth-bound life we know. It is such a dramatic moment in the life of Jesus, and such a dramatic pledge to Christians about their future beyond time. The Lord tells Martha that he can not only restore her brother to life in this world; he can raise anyone who believes in him to the

heavenly life beyond space and time. Surely it is uplifting for us to
live our lives in Christ now, knowing what a glorious future lies ahead
of us with him in glory! The grave ends nothing for the Christian!

Our Lord's words invite a contrast. The contrast is between
how the committed followers of Jesus "read" this thing called life, and
how others have to "read" it without benefit of Jesus.

Many of our neighbors, afflicted by their loss of faith or by
their exhausting workaday lives, may see life as Macbeth saw it—
"a walking shadow," with not much rhyme or reason to it. Job, in the
Bible, saw life as tragic, but still his most prized possession. George
M. Cohan, a songwriter from the early years of the twentieth century,
thought life was "a funny proposition," while Dr. Samuel Johnson reads
it as "a play." James Joyce saw life as the arena where we keep meeting ourselves in others. Hans Christian Andersen saw it as "a fairytale,"
while Eugene F. Ware said it was "a game of whist." An anonymous
scribe called life "a jigsaw puzzle with most of the pieces missing."
I do not doubt that, without Christ, most of us would find our experience of life in one or other of those remarks. But Christ changes
everything for us!

We Christians share a common existence with everyone else
in our society. We come up against the same challenges and questions
as they do. But our life in Christ diverges radically from life as many
others see it—and must experience it—without him. It diverges
because Christ adds two levels to life.

First, the Christian owns something called "new life in Christ"
(see Romans 6:4), other people do not. Saint Paul speaks of it as
a resurrection from the dead even now as we live in this world. He
means that the Christian is one who has been raised from the death of
sin to new life in Christ. It is a new life that clothes the Christian with
grace, with purpose, with values, with the knowledge of the right
priorities in life, and with the mind of Christ that is able to put meaning
into every aspect of ordinary living. Life, with Christ, becomes anything but a "walking shadow." Paul said, "Yet I live, no longer, but Christ
lives in me . . ." (Galatians 2:20).

Second, the Christian does not die. In Christ, the Christian
cannot die. Today's Gospel has the astounding Good News: "I am
the resurrection and the life; whoever believes in me, even if he dies,
will live and everyone who lives and believes in me will never die."

Do I believe this? Yes, I do. Why? Because I have come to believe, as Martha came to believe, that Jesus is the Lord of all history and of all life, and of a new form of life beyond history. Specifically, I accept him as the Lord of my history and of my life, and of what is beyond them for me. I do this because, by his cross, he has proved his love for me; and in his Resurrection he has proved the death-shattering power of his grace for me. And he has proved them for you too.

37A Palm Sunday of the Lord's Passion

At the Procession with Palms

MATTHEW 21:1–11

Triumph and Humility

The central Gospel of this day is, of course, the Passion narrative. But we will look here at this shorter Gospel of the Lord's triumphal entry into Jerusalem. It is the Gospel that is proclaimed at the blessing of the palms.

It can be called the Gospel of the Lord's triumph. In G. K. Chesterton's poem *(The Donkey)*, even the donkey—the lowly beast of burden—is exalted along with Jesus. For one great moment, he hears "a shout about my ears" and sees "the palms before my feet." The humble Lord is exalted too. He is that other lowly one (of Isaiah's vision) who carries on his back the burden of our sins. In this, he is humbled; for this, he is exalted.

So, it is a Gospel of triumph. Yet some holy souls read this Gospel as really a story about the Lord's great humility. Here is their spiritual interpretation. Jesus is Israel's greatest son, and today he should enter his city in triumph. He has more right than any Herod or Caesar to enter Jerusalem in glory. He is of David's house and lineage. He is the reason why God set up David's house in the first place. God set up the house of David so that from it the Savior would come. Jesus is God's only-begotten Son, and Jerusalem is God's city. Jesus is heir to Jerusalem, and to all that it represents. Yet, look at who and what is not present at his triumphal procession into it!

Among the crowds that greet Jesus, there is no welcoming court of Herod. The Sanhedrin and the ruling parties are not there either. There is no guard of honor. In fact, no one who is anyone is there! An emperor always rides a white stallion in his triumphal entry into a city: Jesus rides a lowly donkey. Triumphal streets are normally decked with garlands and flower petals donated by the rich: our Lord's way is lined by the poor with branches from the commonest tree of the wayside, the ubiquitous Middle East palm. City fathers and fat merchants throw their cloaks in gratitude under the stallion's prancing feet: the poor have only their homespun cloaks to throw under the donkey's unshod feet. In this spiritual estimate, the scene on Palm Sunday is anything but a triumph and an exaltation of Jesus. Instead, it is a marvel of humility.

It is one more page in the long story of what the old spiritual commentators call Jesus' self-emptying. He empties himself; he humbles himself in this scene, on our behalf and because of our sins. If this Gospel traditionally marks the start of Holy Week, then our Lord's entry today is the beginning part of the story of his Passion and death—and of His self-emptying. We may thus interpret it as a Gospel of humility.

On the other hand, I think it is more properly a Gospel of triumph. It is the teeming crowd, the mass of poor people, who ought to determine for us what the interpretation should be. Triumph, not the Lord's humiliation, is their intention as they shout their hosannas; as they bless the one "who comes in the name of the Lord God"; and as they bow their palm fronds in deference before him. They are true Israelites, for all their poverty, and they know their scriptures. The greetings they shout at Jesus are all greetings of praise from Psalm 118. In our Bibles, Psalm 118 is entitled "A Hymn of Thanksgiving to the Savior of Israel." The crowds, at this moment, hail Jesus as Israel's Savior even if, a few days later, they will not understand why the Savior of Israel's triumph must end in suffering and death.

But how does a donkey fit into this scene of triumph? Our Lord deliberately chooses a donkey to ride on. He intends this seemingly humiliating choice, not as a lesson in humility as such, but as a messianic statement about himself. In choosing a donkey to ride on, he is realizing the messianic prophecy of the prophet Zechariah, "Rejoice heartily, O daughter Zion, shout for joy, O daughter Jerusalem! See, your king shall come to you; a just Savior is he, meek, and riding on an ass" (Zechariah 9:9).

Today's Gospel presents us with an insight into the messiahship of Jesus as he understood it. It is a *saving* messiahship. The Messiah's role is a *spiritually* saving role as opposed to a political one in the usual sense. For a Savior-Messiah the core issue is always sin, and the breaking of the rule of sin over the human heart and in society. Jesus is the lowly Messiah, the beast of burden, who carries the weight of human sin to the absolution of the cross. Only *after* the cross can the eschatological dimension of his messiahship happen. Then, messiahship becomes God's glorious reign of justice, peace, and love over those now-redeemed hearts and in their new society.

We, in this age of the loss of the sense of sin, have the coming Holy Week to settle this matter of sin decisively between ourselves and our Messiah-Savior.

39ABC Holy Thursday

Evening Mass of the Lord's Supper

JOHN 13:1–15

The Gospel of Service

Some years ago, a bank I did business with hit on a new sales pitch: "Service is our most important product." That line ought to stand as a golden rule among Christians. It certainly was a golden rule with Jesus.

On the religious level, our Lord is celebrating Passover with his disciples, and he is about to institute the momentous ritual that we call the Mass or the Eucharistic Liturgy. On the personal level, he is about to pass from this world to the Father. At such a critical time,

when he should be absorbed in these matters, what does he do?
He starts washing feet!

If this were a stage play, the audience would be intrigued
by the sudden shift in the plot. It has no apparent relationship with
what has been unfolding thus far in the drama of the Passover
celebration. It is an about-face, something entirely unexpected. But,
obviously, Jesus knew what he was doing—and he intended this change,
and this dramatic turn of events, to underline a critical Christian
teaching. The teaching is this: service is our most important product.
A Christian is born to serve.

Our Lord teaches by doing. *He* picks up the basin. *He* pours
the water into it. *He* bends down. *He* does the washing. *He* does the
drying. There is no pious pep talk here, nor stylized ritual. Our Lord's
actions *are* his words. He finishes and asks, "Do you realize what I
have done to you? You call me 'teacher' and 'master,' and rightly so, for
indeed I am. If I, master and teacher, have washed your feet, you ought
to wash one another's feet." If we do not understand the centrality of
service in the life of the Christian, then "you will have no inheritance
with me."

Our own lives, on the contrary, are full of scrambling for
recognition. We are miffed when others do not give us the deference
due our titles, or the place of honor our dignity assumes it deserves.
We are all caught up in the "pecking order" syndrome. Everyone wants
to be served; many have no great desire to serve. It infects even the
Church. Theologian William Barclay observed: "So often, even
in churches, trouble arises because someone does not get his place.
So often even ecclesiastical dignitaries are offended because they
did not receive the precedence to which their office 'entitled' them.
Here [in this Gospel] is the lesson that there is only one kind of
greatness, the greatness of service. The world is full of people who are
standing on their dignity when they ought to be kneeling at the feet
of their brethren."

I don't want us to hear these words, nod our heads in pious
agreement, and go away saying, "What a nice thought!" I want us
to believe it in the way Jesus believed it—by *doing* it as he, our Lord
and Master, did as an example for us.

40ABC Good Friday of the Lord's Passion

JOHN 18:1–19:42

Were You There?

All great creative literature reflects human life and the human condition. The great novels and short stories hinge on characterization, plot, confrontation, conscience, and choice. We find ourselves in the characters of these novels and stories, and in the life situations they find themselves in. We also find ourselves on the pages of that other great corpus of literature, the scriptures.

And so, we find ourselves in one or other of the characters that make up the great drama of Good Friday. When I was a student, the French priest Louis Evely wrote about the Passion and death of Jesus in that manner, and my reflections here are partly a copy of what I remember from him.

What part do you and I play in this tragedy that is the Passion and death of Jesus? We say, excusing ourselves, that we weren't there, that it all happened two thousand years ago. But Calvary goes on every day. It is repeated every day in some faraway dictatorship and also in our own country; in vast cities like Los Angeles, New York, and Chicago and in the small towns of rural America; in drug-infested inner-city families *and* in the family we are part of. We may say that we weren't at the original Calvary and, therefore, played no part in the historical suffering and death of Jesus, but we can *not* say that Calvary does not repeat itself in one form or another in every generation, including our own, and we can *not* avoid playing a part in its modern versions.

What part do I play in the drama? Am I Peter, denying my faith in the office or in the warehouse because I lack backbone? Am I Pilate, washing my hands of a decision that demands justice because I'm afraid to upset the higher-ups in my company and in my Church? Am I the fickle mob that shouts, "Crucify him! Crucify him!"

when a homeless shelter tries to locate in my neighborhood? Am I the culturally conditioned soldier who readily mocks and taunts the homeless panhandlers under the crosses of their agony? Am I the cowardly disciples who flee when the going gets too rough with people of color coming into the neighborhood?

Or, am I the weeping women of Jerusalem who can empathize with a victim because I have a nurturing heart? Am I the legendary Veronica who has the guts to do something and, because of which, I find an impression of Jesus and a grace left on my soul? Am I Simon of Cyrene, no hero and not quite sure what political correctness in the situation calls for, but I let goodness get the better of me? Am I Joseph of Arimathea who risks my social position or my Church position because my heart is human? Am I Mary, the mother, who picks up the pieces of a life shattered by the blindness and the bigotry of others? When I see today's version of the Victim of Calvary (the poor, the homeless, the hungry), do my eyes pass over his and her head as though he and she were not there, or do my eyes meet theirs, and answer their pain?

Sometimes I wonder if the reality of Calvary Past and the challenge of Calvary Present are softened, rather than sharpened, in us when we sing the touching lines of "Were You There When They Crucified My Lord?" and when we conduct our devout ritual of Good Friday. I don't wish to undermine the value of either. I only wonder, and I only raise this question in order to underline a critical pastoral point. It is this: it would be a real tragedy for us if we thought that Calvary and its Victim and its cast of characters appeared only once in human history, and that a long, long time ago.

Easter

42ABC Easter Sunday

The Resurrection of the Lord
The Mass of Easter Day

MATTHEW 28:1–10

Emptying Tombs

We have followed the terrible Passion and death of Jesus in the liturgy during the past week. Part of our journey through his suffering and death was the challenge we received to identify where we stand on the issue of Calvary. Do we stand with Jesus or against him? Are we Veronica and Simon and the Jerusalem women who helped him on the way? Are we the howling mob, and the hand-washing Pilate, and the weak disciples who only hurt him?

We have moved with Jesus, and with that question, through the Passion and death. Now we must move with Jesus from the tomb to the Resurrection, and with another question: the Lord has risen from his tomb; have we risen from ours? The disciple Christian says to himself and herself: "My Lord has risen and is alive. But have I risen from the depth of my sins, and am I alive with his grace on this glorious day?" If you and I have not risen from our own tombs, then the Resurrection of the Lord from his tomb has no meaning in time or in eternity for us.

There are Christians in all our parishes whose joylessness and gloom contradict their belief in the Resurrection. They go about their religious and social lives as though they were being crushed perpetually by the stone at the entrance to Jesus' tomb. So many others continue to live in the tomb of sin, the tomb of drink, the tomb of addiction, the tomb of violence, or the tomb of bad memories from which they despair of ever coming out. They have grown accustomed to their tombs. They are afraid someone may come along and roll back the stone from their tombs, and expose them to the light and the challenge of living a resurrected life.

There still are Christians who turn their homes into tombs for their spouses and their children because of their selfishness and abuse. There are teens and adults by the hundreds of thousands in the lands of the so-called "Christian West" who prefer entombment with drink, drugs, racial fear, violence, and thuggery of various kinds to resurrection with the Lord and real living. They, too, celebrate Easter, but for some unsure reason.

On this glorious day of the Lord, we are sure in faith that he is alive and well. We look forward, like him, to the day when we go back to the Father in glory. In looking forward, we are also looking back at what many of us have left behind. Christians of the present time and of the past two thousand or so years have left behind a vast assortment of tombs. Each in his own way and each through her own response has faced the question: "My Lord lives; do I?" And they have been able to answer: "Yes, Lord! I have walked my passion and my pain in solidarity with yours. I have been lifted high above the hills of my sins. I have emptied my tomb. I, too, am resurrected, and I am alive and well with you on this great day."

43A Second Sunday of Easter

Divine Mercy Sunday

JOHN 20:19–31

Making a Case for Christ

Today's Gospel is part of the Resurrection appearances of Jesus. The Resurrection appearances are, indeed, placed in the Gospels as "proofs" of the Lord's Resurrection. And these "proofs" form an important part of the case for Jesus. "Proofs" (or "showings," as the scholars prefer) were the function of these Resurrection appearances in the early Church's Gospel proclamation to the unchurched, and in its faith catechesis to the churched.

There is a tendency today, in catechetics, to ignore the reasoning or "proof" aspect of our faith. We do not make an intellectually competitive case for Jesus anymore. We excuse ourselves by saying that faith is a gift, and that people either have it or they don't. Faith is, of course, ultimately a gift. But that does not excuse us, it seems to me, from trying to lead people to faith, and from "selling" the Lord—with "proofs"—as best we can in the modern marketplace of competing ideologies.

I think that making a case for Christ has become an imperative for us in our third millennial, quasi-agnostic Western world. Today's Gospel shows Jesus at the task of "proving" himself to others—and, thereby, eliciting faith in doubting Thomas.

Thomas was a witness to three years of proofs about Jesus. He was a part of the Lord's ministry and witnessed his many miracles. Yet he still needed today's Gospel encounter with Jesus. And Jesus did not fail him. Are not the modern mindset and our over-secularizing culture more in need of witnessing and of intelligent evangelization?

Our Holy Father has already given the green light of clear prioritization for a new evangelization. Our local bishops have urged us to evangelize in this new millennium. Will we rely on our local diocesan office of divine worship before we start making the case for Jesus in our own declining parishes and in our communities, in the places we are directly responsible for?

Many years ago, I was responsible for communications in Los Angeles. A man called up demanding to speak to the cardinal. He was incensed that there was no official Church boycott of the Nikos Katzanzakis movie, *The Last Temptation of Christ.* He also had a list of prior "silences" on the part of the official Church in regard to various anti-Catholic organizations, radio programs, and pamphlets.

"What are you Roman-collared people doing about it? What are the cardinal and his bishops doing while our children are poisoned by this filth? Are they out all the time playing golf?" I had the grace to ask in my turn, "What are you doing about it? *Your* children should not be out at night at 'R' rated movies, and *you* are responsible for shepherding *your* own children, and for what they hear, read, and are tempted by in *your* home."

But I did not leave it at that. I started writing reviews of controversial movies in our archdiocesan newspaper, serving on a community

standards movie preview board, and encouraging the clergy of the
mainline Christian churches to oppose the anti-Catholic pamphleteer-
ing of some evangelical Christians.

Making the case for Jesus can take as many, or as few, forms
as local needs dictate. We should not be silent and waiting on others
to do the job for us. All sorts of other voices are out there at work
among the people. If you think the fascination with Tarot cards and
astrology is only a fad, think again! If you think our faith is guaranteed
just because we are baptized, look at the hedged, cherry-picked faith
and "cafeteria" Catholics all around you! Saint Paul tells us that faith is
neither given nor retained purely as gift from above. Intermediaries are
involved. That is why he exhausted himself trying to spread the faith
among nonbelievers and trying to retain it in the converts he had made.
Jesus uses *us* as his instruments in faith's cause. Faith has to be preached
to others and then reinforced in them, "as if God were appealing
through us" (2 Corinthians 5:20).

Do we feel that the task is beyond us? If so, we are not alone.
The Spirit moves the willing heart and directs it in the ways and
means of evangelization that a parish or a community requires.

And the Spirit also moves the same willing heart to a better
alignment of itself with the Gospel that it wants to preach to others.
For in the final analysis, it is not our academic degrees and pastoral
strategies, our synods and our workshops that matter, important though
they be; it is the messenger's own faithful life in Christ that speaks
loudest and best. I believe it was Saint Philip Neri who first coined the
expression, "I am conscious that I may be the only copy of the gospels
some people will ever read."

46A Third Sunday of Easter

LUKE 24:13−35

A Grammar of the Lord's Presence

This is one of the most attractive scenes in the Bible. It speaks of
the presence, the sensitive presence, of Jesus with us even when we
think he's absent. It also tells us that our Lord can make sense of the
nonsense of life and of the obstacles we encounter in our personal
lives. All of life can be read with the mind of Jesus. Life makes sense
only with the mind and heart of Jesus.

The two disciples are going home to Emmaus from Jerusalem.
They have just experienced the death of Jesus and the collapse of
their dream. He's gone. He's dead and buried. The dream is finished.
It is all over. Now they face a difficult future. Their faith is shattered.
They have wasted three years of their lives on a false Messiah.
Did they also leave wife and children and farm to follow him, as he
once asked? (see Matthew 19:29). Their neighbors will taunt them
as losers. They hitched their chariot to a falling star. Fools! No
wonder the scripture says that they are downcast and in a state
of lively argumentation over the events that happened in Jerusalem
and on Calvary.

Suddenly, a stranger joins them. It is Jesus, but they do not
recognize him. He explains to them, gently and at great length, how
the Messiah had first to suffer and die. It is only through this sacrifice
of love that the Messiah could fulfill his destiny. They are so taken
with the stranger, and with his explanation of their predicament, that
they invite him to stay with them as the night draws nigh. He is a
charming and an illuminating teacher. How much more in their lives
might he not shed light on! They know by now that he is someone
who can cut through their night and fog of human existence. He makes
sense of everything. He sheds the light of God on it.

They sit for an evening meal. In the course of the meal, Jesus
does something familiar. He "took bread, said the blessing, broke it,
and gave it to them," as he had done so often before for them, and as

he had done, but with such a different and fuller meaning, at the Last Supper. They recognize their stranger in the breaking of the bread. It is their Jesus!

Why did they not recognize him before this moment? One scholar says it's because the sun was in their eyes on the road; for Emmaus is west of Jerusalem, and they were walking into the blinding glare of a Palestinian sunset. I think myself that they had trouble recognizing him—as had all the apostles during the Lord's post-Resurrection appearances—because he was changed, in some brilliant way, by the glory of his Resurrection.

I learn a lesson about the presence of God from this story. I learn that Jesus is always with me even when his presence is hidden from me. The Emmaus story is, of course, from the evangelist's point of view, a "proof" story of the Resurrection of Jesus. That was the evangelist's intention in recording it in his Gospel. But the story speaks equally to our pastoral need today. It is not only an assurance of the Resurrection, but an assurance of God's abiding presence with us in an age in which God, like so many Catholics, is said to have been missing. It's all about God's presence with us through Jesus, and about the quality of his presence, even in an age said to be suffering from an absent and silent God.

The story of what happened on the Emmaus road is a sort of grammar of the Lord's presence. It tells us that our Lord is always *spiritually* present with us even though he is physically absent. He is aware of the two disciples, and of their pain, even before he comes physically into their journey. He is aware of ours, too, and all the time. The story then tells us that our Lord is always *scripturally* present with us in the life-giving words that speak to us of him and that, in our breaking open of those words, speak to the whole range of our human-ity and to our personal experiences whether good and bad. Then the story tells us that our Lord is eucharistically present with us through the eucharistic liturgy that unites us to him as one body. And, finally, the story tells us that our Lord is present with us in the assured *hope* of glory that his Resurrection is a pledge of, the hope that was re-ignited by the stranger in the two disciples, and that set their hearts on fire within them.

This hope of future glory is assured. Jesus returned to these disciples on their way to Emmaus after his Resurrection, just as he had promised. He made a promise to us too. He said he would come back to take us with him, so that where he now is we also may be (see John 14:1–3). Even now, at this moment, he is returning to us—coming to meet us out of the future even as we journey in time to meet him.

49A Fourth Sunday of Easter

John 10:1–10

Shepherd and Sheep

I was once visiting a friend on a farm in western Illinois. It was well off the interstate and far enough away from the town and traffic where you could really hear the silence. Since my friend is a sheep farmer, there were hundreds of sheep in the fields around his home. On some of the more carefree mornings, I would enjoy watching them while my friend was out on the "south forty." I grew to love them, for all their legendary dumbness! They grazed the fields around the house and, now and then, a few would wander onto the yard between the barn and house as they were being moved down the road from field to field.

During a visit one March, a ewe and her lamb wandered in. The mother just stopped cold when she saw me. She looked at me with a sort of disbelief. I don't think she sensed she was in the wrong place. I think she sensed that I didn't belong in this picture. I was unfamiliar. I was a stranger. I spoke to her. But my voice only seemed to mystify her all the more. Finally, she turned away. It reminded me of a line in today's Gospel: "They will not follow a stranger; they will run away from him, because they do not recognize the voice of strangers."

Sheep dominated Judea in Jesus' time, as they had done throughout the biblical generations. Judea was not a set of neat, continuous fields of short green grass like my rural Ireland. It may have been known as sheep country, but it was very rugged sheep country. The grassland was patchy, with entangling scrub and briers. Rocks and crags and crevasses were plentiful. So were wolves and rustlers, and flash floods that could sweep the sheep away. A Judean shepherd had to be totally committed to his flock. And he was.

That is why, I suppose, the shepherd entered Jewish theology as a template of God. And that, I suppose, is why Jesus came to say that he is "the good shepherd" who "lays down his life for his sheep." His hearers readily understood what he meant.

The experts tell us that Judean sheep actually knew their shepherd's voice, and that they followed it. They would follow no other voice but his. Sheepdogs were not used. Neither were the whistles one hears today at sheepdog trials. The Judean shepherd spoke to his sheep. He gave each one a name, and he called it and spoke to it by name. It all suggests a great familiarity, and a great loyalty, between the shepherd and his flock. I believe our Lord is using these facts as illustration of his commitment to us as his special flock—even down to the detail of knowing each of us, and calling each of us by name. That is an aspect of the religious relationship that we should savor with delight.

In addition, there is a challenge in this Gospel for us. On one level, we are the Lord's flock and his loving responsibility. On another level, we are all shepherds, each of us responsible for a flock of our own. The parish priest has his flock. The mom and dad have their flock. My neighbors on the street, and the people with whom I work, and the kids in my classroom are my flock.

And then there's my own personal life. I am responsible for giving it a proper Christian shepherding. Am I allowing Jesus, the good shepherd, to be the real shepherd in my life or have other "voices" become more attractive to me? For example, does Christ have to compete with TV and MTV, with economic goals and pet projects, with raves and events, even, mind you, with frantic good works and too many community and church organizations, for space in my life? Or do I adjust these concerns to my life in such a way that they are truly useful to my well-being and to the well-being of others, and in a way that they never force me to lose the hearing of Christ the good shepherd calling my name?

In our Church's view, the Lord does most of his shepherding through word and sacrament. Many Catholics today are absent from their parish church and, therefore, from this key form of their Lord's shepherding. Like good shepherds, we must not lose heart.

We must keep after any dropouts that we know of. We must call them by name to an understanding of the Church's importance in their lives. They are missing so much in missing the Church's shepherding. And they are not finding its replacement on the edge or in the stars.

52A Fifth Sunday of Easter

JOHN 14:1–12

Show Us God!

Ask young people what their problem is with God and they will tell you: "I don't know if He's there. I've never seen Him. He's all too vague. He never shows himself. When He didn't stop Hitler and the death camps, how can you talk about Him? And He wasn't there for the abused children either. I wouldn't say it to your face because I know you, but I'll tell you what a lot of my generation thinks: You priests shed no useful light on Him. You just go through the motions."

A lot of things are hidden in those words, and a full response to them would take us into psychology as much as into religion. That is not our mandate for the pulpit. Enough is theologically clear. People are out there and they cannot find two things. One is the key to the understanding of God, and the other is the handle on life.

The young people I speak with are not godless or antireligious as such. They are just frustrated with a God who doesn't show Himself, and with a Church that seems to shed no useful light on Him. They express emotionally what science and psychology express coldly and objectively: We haven't found God in the outer reaches of the universe or in the inner depths of the human psyche. "If God exists," said the philosopher and mathematician Bertrand Russell, "he has not given us enough signs of himself" *(Why I Am Not a Christian)*. Jesus says he has. If young people are to know God, and to put meaning into their lives, it is best to try to bring them to Jesus. Jesus has revealed God, and explained the meaning of life, as no other in history has.

Philip said, "Master, show us the Father and that will be enough for us." Jesus replied, "Whoever has seen me has seen the Father." Jesus meant it quite literally. For Jesus is the "the very imprint of his being" (Hebrews 1:3) or, to use the modern language of genetics, Jesus is the precise image and replication of God. I do not know how God could possibly make Himself more visible and more understandable to human beings than by taking on a human form and body, and then walking among us in our history as Jesus of Nazareth. He was here in history two thousand years ago for the human race to see. The record of that incarnation is there now in the Gospels for all of us to read, and the Spirit that Jesus sent is here today, as pursuing grace, for every seeking heart to find and to be comforted by.

In Jesus, we see not only God visible and tangible, but we see the whole range of what is within God, and what makes God tick. God uncovers Himself in Jesus with a mind and instincts and emotions and dreams and hopes that parallel the best of our own. His mindset is on humility, rather than on majesty. He is the God who created amazing galaxies and constellations, but who finds the creation of a graced human heart a matter of greater concern and joy to Him. He is the God of power, but it is the power of healing and of saving miracle that concerns Him most. He is the God of justice, but even more of mercy. He is the God who reads minds in order to comfort hearts. We see all of this, and this entire God, in Jesus.

God, in Jesus, said that he is the good shepherd who would leave all and go out and search for one lost sheep and, when he found it, carry it back in triumph on his shoulders. He never said, "If I find it." He always knew he would. Not because he was clairvoyant but because his love was so compelling. He said that he would lay down his life for love of us. And one day, on Calvary, he did.

What did Jesus think when all of his showing to us of God's mind and greater heart only earned him death by our hand? It is clear enough from the Gospels that Jesus accepted his death for our sins as the expression of God's undying love for us.

What is not equally clear, in my mind at any rate, is how any of us can be excused for walking around and talking about an unknown God, when we don't bother to look with open eyes into the face of Christ in order to see and know the living and loving God.

55A Sixth Sunday of Easter

JOHN 14:15–21

Tolerance

Like many others, I have preached on this Gospel before. Like many others, I have used this Gospel to underline the Church's teaching authority. The Spirit of truth is given to the Church. The Church, therefore, "possesses" God's truth. When we preach this way we tend to restrict the meaning of truth, and the range of the Spirit's action, to Church dogma and the Church's magisterium.

The Church does, indeed, speak God's truth in the power of the Spirit. And the Church is spoken to—consolingly and encouragingly—by this advocate Spirit. But the Church is also spoken to, in a confrontational or charismatic way, by the same Spirit. The Church is not always open to this particular adversarial voice, even though the holy adversarial voice is always a reforming and a renewing one. I think that the Spirit is speaking a truth to us today as Church, *as the local parish church,* and it is an adversarial truth. Let us not be afraid to face it head on. It is the Lord who speaks.

You and I are the Church, you and I as this parish and as this community. Communities like ours must face the confrontational and charismatic voice of the Spirit in many ways. For example, immigrants arrive in our community frequently. This can be disturbing as we try to adjust to new neighbors. It's not that our community is racist or elitist. Hopefully, we are neither, thank God. And we have no intention of becoming such. But we must come to grips with the fact that there could be strangers in our midst. And it is all new to some of us—even though we are a nation if immigrants.

Instead, let us raise our sights a little higher, and face the challenges because we follow Jesus. The immigrants in our community came here to find better lives for themselves and their families. And as Catholics, we are therefore pledged to Christ and to his standards. All of us are pledged to each other as God's children. We are a nation made up of immigrants. Given this ancestry, only the best should be expected of us by those who are in need today.

In the Gospel, the Spirit of God is called an advocate. An advocate is someone who pleads on behalf of another. The Spirit is *our* advocate with God, for sure. But he is also, now, *their* advocate with us. Therefore, you and I will not stop our ears in the presence of the pleading Spirit. The Spirit is pleading for our patience, for the withholding of prejudgment, for understanding, for tolerance, and for the spirit of active brotherly and sisterly love in Christ.

Therefore, we will not speak to the immigrants the hard words of a world that Jesus says "does not see nor recognize" the Spirit of God. We will be the voice and the hands and heart of Jesus to them, knowing that his words were spoken to them as much as to us when he said, "I will not leave you orphans" (John 14:18).

58A The Ascension of the Lord

MATTHEW 28:16–20

Way to Go!

There are two "goings" in this Gospel. First of all, there is our Lord's Ascension, his going back to the Father. It is a glorious going. As Luke's Gospel puts it, "he was taken up to heaven" (Luke 24:51).

Many people today don't want to go, to ascend to the Father, at least not yet! Life is familiar. Life today is quite cozy. In fact, it has never been better, materially speaking, for the human family in our country. Faith is, correspondingly, weak. The end is not attractive at all. Death is in a state of denial in our Western world, and we wish to give it as long a postponement as we can possibly can. We have more reasons than ever before to agree with Hamlet that it is better to stay with this comfortable world that we know "than fly to others that we know not of" *(Hamlet,* 3.1*).*

And yet, for Jesus, going to heaven, being taken up in a rapture of glory is a joy, and it is the culmination of his faith-filled life.

It's the only way to go! And it is the same joy that all of us, who follow him in this life, may look forward to at the end. The unbelieving world may have to live staring "dismal death" in the face. We live facing death as glory.

The second "going" in this Gospel is the great commission; the sending forth of the disciples to convert the nations of the earth to a life of faith in Jesus, with its promise of glory. "Go, make disciples of all the nations."

This particular "going" is also in a state of denial in our Western world. We haven't the heart to seek converts with anything like the vigor of the past. And many people don't want to hear the Lord's words of life or the message of the Church anymore. Is it because the one has damaged the other? Has the Church lost its right, in society's eyes, to speak for Christ anymore because of its sins? Has Christ *himself* lost his right to engage the nations anymore? What has his grace achieved for a world still crippled by abuse and genocide, war and want? A university professor once said to me, "You and your Christ have had center stage for two thousand years. You haven't done a good job. Now it's time for you to move to the wings and give another philosophy the chance to engage people and to enhance their lives."

I have to speak for myself. But I hope that, in speaking for myself, I might engage some others too. I still believe that the best way to go in this life, and for the next, is Christ's way. I still believe that our society is not fulfilled by its modernity, its technological break-throughs, its sophistication, or its affluence. There is nothing wrong with any of these as such. It's just a question of what is missing from them.

Economics and comfort are not the full measure of what the human heart longs for. Creature comforts and sophistication will not satisfy the spiritual hunger of the heart. People sit all day at their computer screens, and many evenings at the bar or before the TV set. They look a bit lost to me. There is only so much that commuting and computing, the East coast and the West coast, the NFL and the NBA, aromatherapy and body toning, the health club and golf rounds "a thousand lost golf balls" (T. S. Eliot), designer drugs and designer sandwiches, sales charts and bottom lines, cell phones, PDAs, and wireless technology can do for any of us. Pleasure may be present, but deep-down joy is missing. Inner peace is missing. The handle on life is missing. The expectation of a joyful future beyond the grave is missing.

Our Lord's going into glory, and our going out to offer his way and its deep-down joy to others are intimately connected. They both address the limitations that people feel in their lives today, and they speak to the unnamed anxiety that many people have, especially the young, because the future they feel in their bones is only a grave with no glory beyond it. And that is how it is going to remain for them without Christ, and without the vision of their own ultimate ascension.

59A Seventh Sunday of Easter

JOHN 17:1–11A

Now Is the Hour

"Now Is the Hour" is the title of an old World War II-era song. Some of us are old enough to have heard it over the radio back then. Those of you who are young may have heard it sung in video documentaries about the war. Now is the hour . . . when her soldier boy must go away to war. But when he returns he'll find her waiting for him. The war is only an interruption of their love. When they are united again, there will be another hour, this time a glorious and unending hour.

In the Gospel for today, Jesus has spent three years in ministry and they are drawing to a close—three years away from the glory he had from all eternity with the Father in heaven; three years of teaching and healing and doing good works for those on earth. He had a job to do on earth. It is completed. So, he says, "Father, the hour has come. Give glory to your son."

You and I will come eventually to that hour, when our pilgrimage here and our time for doing good is over. It will be our final hour of this life but the first hour of our new life in glory. We must stop looking at the end of our earthly journey as the hour of our death. For a Christian, it is anything but. It is the hour of glory.

As it is with Jesus, so it is with us. This hour of glory is born from all those other hours of faith and goodness, of testing and trouble, that fill each ordinary day of the time and the place and the career and the vocation God has put us in. All great athletes train for years so that they may have their hour of glory at the Olympics. Every worthwhile artist rehearses for years, even decades, in the hope of making it to London or Vienna or New York, to the hour of glory. And all, Saint Paul says, "to win a perishable crown" (1 Corinthians 9:25). You and I, he continues, are after "an imperishable crown." "Run then," he says, "so as to win!" (v. 24).

Now is my appointed hour! Now is my hour in service to others and in worship of God. Now is my hour in marriage and in education, in opportunity for kindness and in possibility of influence. Now is my hour in learning discipleship from Jesus and in practicing discipleship so that my hour for glory later may be all the more assured and all the more intense. We should grasp this hour, this short time before glory, for the opportunities it offers us.

Do not say that we don't know how to use it. Jesus said, "Learn from me" (Matthew 11:29). This we do by reading the Gospels with openness, and then discerning where Jesus' words and actions may find their parallel in our own lives and in ministry. He is our model for personal living, and our pattern for dealing with others. He teaches us how to use the hour. Do not say that we are insignificant; that we are too small; that we have no power for good or evil. Each of us has significant power in his and her own sphere through the way we teach others, the way we influence others for good or bad, and in the way we are concerned and caring or cold and callous.

How some of us wish for another hour!—a different ministry, another marriage, a better town, a better talent, a more visible and influential presence with peers! What a waste of our hour! God has written His image in us, and He has fashioned the particular person that is you or me, and not someone else.

He has set me into this time, this culture, this environment, and this set of opportunities as He eternally conceived them for me. He has given me my hour with its unique pain and promise, its appointed persons and their needs, its challenges, its opportunities, and also its graces.

We live in our hour of history by divine appointment. We will not be located here again or walk this way again. We will not be given the years back again. We cannot erase the people given by God to our time and place, to our care, concern, and ministry in our hour. Their names are written alongside ours for good or ill in the book of life or the book of loss. This is it for you and for me! Now is our hour in ministry! Let us fill it with light and life and love, so that our hour for glory can do nothing else but infallibly follow it.

63A Pentecost Sunday

Mass during the Day

JOHN 20:19–23

Casting Fire

In the Gospel for the feast of the Ascension, the Church is given the great commission of making disciples of all the nations. It was Jesus' work. It now becomes the Church's work. In the Gospel for Pentecost, the Church is given the power of forgiving sins and making people right before God. It was the Lord's work. It now becomes the Church's work. Indeed, the whole ministry of the Lord is turned over to the Church. But, of course, the ministry remains the Lord's ministry, for he and the Church make up one and the same body.

Jesus once said, "I have come to set the earth on fire, and how I wish it were already blazing!" (Luke 12:49). He began the task so well! Now, we must continue it! It was not interrupted by his death: it is further empowered by his death. His return to glory only adds immeasurable strength and grace to the effort. It is up to us to catch the new Spirit and to cast the fire.

I always tire of politicians who want us to elect them so that our children and grandchildren will have a better future. I always feel that their motives are suspect. I'm a firm believer in making our leaders take care of *our* generation, *our* time and its challenges, and that we should not allow them to deflect our minds to some vague future that can only be grounded usefully on the performance of the present.

I suspect that there are Church leaders who likewise "cast their anchor" into the future rather than taking care of the present. They write off the present generation and look instead, like politicians, to the future. They say things are bad now, what with the scarcity of vocations, the departures from the priesthood, the scandals, the affluence, the false values, the hedonism, the violence, the egotism, and the lack of a generous heart. But the future will be different! So, we must look to the future, side-stepping the present. They are wrong. They are appointed to be the shepherds of the present, and not of some vague future. The future is someone else's responsibility.

I heard one young priest say, "I'll give it (the ministry) a try for a few years and see what happens." Another said to me, "If they (the people) don't come to church, it's their problem, not mine." I was part of a discussion with young people where the general feeling about marriage was "It better work from the word *go,* because I'm not hanging around trying to fix it." A teacher said to me, "Trying to teach religion to this generation is like pulling teeth."

I cannot say that I do not understand these sentiments, or that I have no sympathy for those who speak them. I only say that I cannot accept these sentiments as adequate responses to the religious challenges of our own time and place. We must take care of our own time and our own place in salvation history. The great commission means we must—and Pentecost means we can.

We tend to see Pentecost as a mighty rush of the Spirit energizing all things with wonder and light and multiple conversions. And that, surely, is part of it. But Pentecost is also the quiet breath of the Spirit, speaking calmly within us about our unmoored time, keeping us strong in faith and anchored in the present as we wonder about the next step, informing our minds with possible solutions and new pastoral approaches, and assuring our hearts that personal holiness is the most effective catechesis of all. No generation— the present one included—is able to withstand the witness of saints. Does the present generation see sanctity in the present set of shepherds? Or does it see shepherds looking to the future, side-stepping the present?

Is *that* what we are called to in our own time and place? Is *that* the challenge of this generation to us—to be saints—to witness to them by our holiness? If it is, and if we achieve it with God's grace, then—and then only—may we happily write off this generation for a spiritual poverty of its own making. But, until we are well on the way to holiness, write off nothing and don't expect too much!

Ordinary Time

64A Second Sunday in Ordinary Time

JOHN 1:29–34

The Lamb of God

President Franklin Delano Roosevelt, as you well know from your history studies, called the day of the Japanese attack on Pearl Harbor "a date which will live in infamy." It was a sneak attack on the U.S. military, infamous because war had not been declared by either side in accordance with law. All the more infamous must be rated the sneak attack on the World Trade Center in lower Manhattan. There was no prior wrangling among diplomats and no prior rattling of sabers to signal danger, as had occurred prior to Pearl Harbor, and more souls were lost in New York than at Pearl Harbor, and all of the victims, civilian.

The dead of Pearl Harbor and of the World Trade Center were victims in the true sense of the word. We mourn them still, and we will continue to keep them in our hearts and in our prayers. There is something unforgettable about the image of young men, some still in their teens, trapped in the steel bowels of the USS *Arizona* with the water rising to drown them and in the TV images of ordinary men and women, just like ourselves, falling like small broken birds from the sky of New York.

Victims come in other and more prevalent forms, too. Every society, and even the Church, has its victims. There are the victims of child abuse and the victims of false accusations and rumors. There are the victims of others' arrogance and power. There are the victims of others' overlooking and under-valuation of them. There are the victims of translation—or the lack of it—where the fine documents and the fine words of institutions never materialize as actions, or only lamely so. All of us live beside victims of street and neighborhood violence or are among the victims ourselves. And, if truth be told, we have done our share of victimization ourselves, however slight we think that victimization was or is. But it all contributes to the wrong cause. Victims! Victims! Victims! We have more than enough of them in history to last us a million years without creating any more of them. Let us be done with victims and victimization! A pious hope, I suppose, but it must be said.

The ultimate victim appears in today's Gospel. John the Baptist points him out: "Behold, the Lamb of God who takes away the sin of the world!" There is Jesus, the one who takes the sin of the world, and who takes our personal history of sin to the cross, and who cancels it out with his blood! He was "like a lamb led to the slaughter or a sheep before the shearers, he was silent and opened not his mouth. Oppressed and condemned, he was taken away . . . and smitten for the sin of his people" (Isaiah 53:7–8).

History is, on one level, the story of victimization. The century we just left behind us was great in scientific achievement, but massive in the range of its victimization. It was a century of genocide, from Armenia at its opening to Africa at its close. It was a century of concentration camps and slave labor camps and extermination camps. It was a century of man-made famines on the grand scale and of man-made economic marginalization of hundreds of millions of God's children. It was a century of wars of liberation, civil wars, turf wars, drug wars, thug wars, and street wars. Victims abounded, whether in or out of uniform.

There were two world wars in which millions of young men in uniform died and tens of millions of ordinary civilians were eliminated by execution, starvation, exposure, carpet bombing, terror bombing, firestorms, atomic radiation, ethnic cleansing and post-war revenge. All of these people were victims in one way or another. Following these victims were the processions of the peacetime victims of shattered economies, joblessness, emigration and the despairing psychology that is built into men and women and children because of them. Late in the century the hidden victims came into the light in great numbers, the victims of chronic sexual and domestic abuse.

Is Christ to go on and on—forever—as the victim in the cynical abuse of the least of his brothers and sisters? Or will we be done with it, once and for all? Go out there and tell the world that this is the kind of history that created the Lamb of God, that crucified the gentle Christ, and the history that continues to crucify him! And tell your own self clearly, once and for all, that a Christian is someone who cannot in conscience create victims.

67A Third Sunday in Ordinary Time

MATTHEW 4:12–23 (LONGER) OR MATTHEW 4:12–17 (SHORTER)

Lighting Up Lives

"It is better to light one candle than to curse the darkness." So said Father Keller, the founder of the Christophers, those Christians who try to contribute something positive, however small, to each situation and in each challenge in daily life. '

Educators use the lighted lamp as the symbol of their profession. It stands for the light of knowledge. The Bible says "a lamp to my feet is your word, a light to my path," that is, my guidance in a murky moral world (Psalm 119:105). In today's Gospel, Matthew says that with the coming of Jesus, "the people who sit in darkness have seen a great light." We are that people, and Jesus is our light.

I think we are all a bit confused today about where to find light in the darkness and how to be a light for others, especially for our children. For example, the whole issue of the religious education of the young is no longer a straightforward one of imparting a Christian worldview, or some Christian values, in the context of a very supportive social environment. That is, more or less, history. Also, in the religious education of many young people there are prior issues standing in the way, issues of motivation and psychology, of anxiety and depression, and drugs, that need the assistance of counseling and therapy before effective catechesis can begin.

The social environment of our time, especially the one that our teenagers inhabit, is not the traditional environment of the normal life-growth challenges. For so many, it is the new environment of urban anxiety and fear, the environment of threat, bullying, and physical danger. It is very difficult for the light of Christ—and your light—to break through such social darkness. So, if we now have an urban generation that is more and more adrift of Christ and the Gospel, we are not casting easy condemnations on the heads of parents or teachers or the youngsters themselves. We wish only to encourage them. Don't give up despite what seem to be the many brick walls in front of you, and the lack of measurable results!

For those of us in less stressed environments, and who are able to be present here at the liturgy, the story is a bit different. So, our challenge from this Gospel is also a bit different. It has nothing to do with breaking through dark social environments and fragile psychologies, but everything to do with re-kindling our own lamp.

So, we ask ourselves some questions: Is Christ still the light of my life? Does he really "light up my life," as the not-so-recent pop song affirms? It's like that other question about the shepherd's voice: Is Christ's voice the one I really listen to, or has it been half-drowned in the competing and confusing voices of others? Is the light of Christ still the dominant light of my life?

Time takes the sheen off things. "The years as they pass plunder one thing after another" (Horace, *Epistles*, 11). The paint fades. The fabric thins. The burnished gold dims. The early enthusiasm for Christ gets tempered. There's hardly anything worse for a Christian than growing old and growing cold in Christ. It was Saint Paul who urged us, "Do not be conquered by evil but conquer evil with good" (Romans 12:21).

In the darkened landscape of weak faith, upscale scams, consumer rip-offs, broken promises, and political cynicism, will I curse the darkness or light a candle? Will I re-kindle the light? The Gospel expects us to see Jesus as a great liberation of light, a liberation from the darkness of the rulers of this world, a liberation from their dark shenanigans and from the darkness of our own sins, confusion, and apathy. Does Christ remain the light of my life, and am I, in turn, still his light to others?

Do we let his light shine on our Sunday church faces but nowhere else? Christ has light to shine on much else: on our business concerns, our romantic concerns, our driving and drinking concerns, our care of the environment concerns, our neighborhood concerns, even our voting concerns. All things should be done in Christ. All concerns should be measured by Christ's measures. All issues should be illuminated with the light of Christ.

It all gets back to the issue of the Epiphany in my life. Is Jesus still the great light of my life and of my salvation? And how well am I, in my turn, bringing his light to all in my sphere of influence, to all whose present-in-Christ and whose future-with-Christ are mysteriously caught up in my own?

70A Fourth Sunday in Ordinary Time

MATTHEW 5:1-12A

Revolutionary Values

These are the beatitudes, the values of the people who live under the moral rule of Jesus in the kingdom of God. Someone has said that the beatitudes are "the charter of Christians." Someone else has said that they can only be lived fully by fools or saints. They are revolutionary values. They turn the normal values of the world upside down.

Hitler thought that they reduced a man to a miserable lump of humanity. Most power-brokers—whether in religious history or secular history—pay only lip service to them. Only saints seem to take them seriously. Was that our Lord's intention? I think not. The beatitudes define the Christian, not just the canonized saint, and God's blessings are upon such a true believer.

Jesus says that the reign of God belongs to the people who follow these beatitudes. I understand his statement in two senses. First, those who practice these values are living the will of God fully in their lives right now. Second, those who practice these values already "own" God's kingdom, both in this life and in the next. They belong. They belong to God. They will always belong to God.

How are we to understand these beatitudes so as to put them into practice and be blessed in them? Several interpretations are possible, conditioned by time, personal mindset, and culture. There is, for example, a traditional spiritual interpretation of the beatitudes. There is also a social justice interpretation. There is a liberation theology interpretation. Then there is the radical interpretation of saints of the caliber of Francis of Assisi. There is the biblical scholars' interpretation. Well, here is a pastoral interpretation:

Those who are poor in spirit are the believers who depend on God for everything. They do not rely on power or privilege or wealth or on their connections. They rely on God alone, and they trust Him absolutely. Our Western affluence gives us many blessings. And we are grateful. But let us remember that economic tigers seldom stay put. God, on the other hand, does. Rely on Him alone, and trust Him absolutely.

The sorrowing are those who endure the awful personal losses of life with faith. And others' losses touch them as deeply as their own. And, in view of the last line about the persecution to come, these sorrowing but blessed ones are the Jesus people who embrace in advance the additional losses that will be demanded of them in the sorrow side of being committed to Christ. We already suffer losses to the faith among our children and friends. These are a form of persecution for us, but we endure it in imitation of the Lord. He died on an almost friendless Calvary.

The lowly are those who are humble in the right sense of that word. They are empty of self and selfishness. As a result, they are like furrows cut in the rich topsoil of the field: they are as open as can be to the word of God. They are ready to grow that word because it is buried in the rich soil of their hearts. Don't let that good topsoil take in the word of empty sophistication in place of the rich word of God!

Blessed are those who hunger and thirst for justice. The actionable verbs—*hungering* and *thirsting*—have a dynamic meaning in scripture. Our Lord is speaking here of believers who yearn, from top to bottom, inside and out, for righteousness and justice. Justice? What is that? The most critical justice in the Bible is justification before God, i.e. our own personal righteousness. It is hungering and thirsting to be right before God, and it is a yearning that all humanity should stand right before God. And, since Jesus joins the first two commandments together in his teaching, we must also include under our hunger for justice the full set of just relationships that one should obtain in the parish, the diocese, the neighborhood, the nation, and the whole earth. So, let us enjoy the good things of God's earth by all means, but let us not hunger and thirst for them as if we could carry creature comfort and gadgetry beyond the grave and into eternal life. We hunger and thirst for justice instead!

Blessed are the merciful, those who live *hesed,* those who show to others the full depth of this Hebrew word. It begins with everyday kindness, and then moves deeper to human understanding, compassion, empathy, and getting inside the other person so as to feel and agonize as that person feels and agonizes, "walking in the other man's moccasins" as it were, and forgiving that person from our deepest level of human understanding and compassion.

The single-hearted? The pure in heart, in some translations? These are the people whose focus on God, and on the love of their neighbor, and on their ministry, and on their obligations of work and family as a single-hearted focus and a singular devotion. There is no lack at all in their dedication, and they do not have mixed motives. Our lists of social and personal sins are, perhaps, sad evidence of the lack of moral focus and single-heartedness among many of us Christians.

The peace makers? It means what we think it means—making peace; creating peace among men and women and in the Church community, in the neighborhood, in the world. Scottish Theologian William Barclay makes a point that is worth attention. This blessing, he says, is not on the peace *lovers,* but on the peace *makers.* It's the difference between nice talk and action on the ground. And peace means all that makes for a person's well-being and for the community's well-being. It is much easier to chain yourself to a government building over a war far away than to chain your heart to a half-way house hoping to locate in the middle of the street where you live.

Blessed are those slandered for Christ's sake. This blessing is not on me because I am slandered by my friends or by my foes; it is on me only if I am slandered because of my allegiance to Christ. Are you and I being sufficiently slandered for Christ today? At work? At play? In the home? Where we socialize? Does our society, which we so often call half-pagan, notice a difference between itself and you and me in the way we vote, and in the values and the priorities we hold? It should.

Blessed are these beatitude people: the kingdom of God belongs to them.

73A Fifth Sunday in Ordinary Time

MATTHEW 5:13–16

You Are the Light

Every coach in the NFL, MBA, or NCAA hopes for a team with "the right stuff." If he or she has such a team, he or she will win the Super Bowl, the World Series, or the NCAA title. "Get out there now guys, and show me the right stuff!"

I'm sure the coach of our faith life, the Holy Spirit, has the same hope and dream for every Christian generation. Jesus spent so much time coaching his disciples, so much time forming them. He's still doing it with our generation through Spirit, word, and sacrament. "You are the salt of the earth! You are the light of the world!" There is a huge responsibility on our shoulders. But there is also Christ's conviction that we can do it with his grace. And we can.

We Christians may groan and say, "We—the salt of the earth, the light of the world? You must be joking! We're only human. We're just poor sinners. How dare we think we are better than others!" Christ dares us to think that we are—but only with his Spirit, word, and grace, of course. It can be done. It has happened many times in history and at least once spectacularly. Tertullian wrote about the early Christians in his work, *Apologeticus.* The pagans, he said, looked at the Christians and said to themselves, "See, these Christians: how they love one another!"

The Christian life stands out like a beacon on a hill to searchers who are stuck in a technologically advanced but spiritually dim world looking for light. Christ and his values shine like a lighted city when seen by confused souls from the valley of the world's frustration and moral darkness. I do not think that we appreciate how important the light of Christ is to so many people lost in our modern world, and how like a revelation his values are to them when they find them.

I, for one, know perfectly well—so do the thousands of missionary priests and religious who went to all parts of the globe with the Gospel, and who have been the channel through which hundreds of thousands have come to Christ after groping for years in the darkness without him. It's a torment to many souls to be out there in the wilderness of a vast, anonymous cityscape like London, Los Angeles, New York, or Chicago without a personal relationship with God, or a moral compass to steer by.

Are many believers, once joyfully baptized as children in one or other of the Christian churches, now also getting lost in our vast cityscapes and even in the quiet backwaters that are not immune to unchristian influences? Are we beginning to get a bit lost ourselves? Here is Jesus in today's Gospel, looking into our eyes, and saying, "You are the salt of the earth. You are the light of the world!"

Questions: First of all, do Jesus and his values still hold as the light that lights up my own personal life? Or have Jesus and his values faded a bit in the strobe and neon lights, the TV screen and the bars and the night clubs, in the flashing faces of celebrities and sundry gurus, in the glint of consumer commercials, and in the warm glow of an easier Western set of values? Is there a Bible or a New Testament at home and, more importantly, do I read it? And do I read it as part of family prayer in that domestic church that is the church of my own home? I and my family need the fashioning of the word of God.

And when I am out there, at work and in community affairs, am I a light of social justice in the parish and in the community? How much am I the "lighted city on the hilltop," professing the values that are specifically Christ's values, values that are in conflict even with some of my friends' values, and values that should cause me pain and loss at least now and then in my life?

76A Sixth Sunday in Ordinary Time

MATTHEW 5:17–37 (LONGER) OR
MATTHEW 5:20–22A, 27–28, 33–34A, 37 (SHORTER)

A More Excellent Way

When I was younger, I always got a bit upset with a certain senior priest in the administration arm of the archdiocese. When a parish wanted to offer a new rehab program, or distribute pro-life material on the sidewalk at the bottom of the church steps, or open the gym to transients in cold weather, he always asked, "Is it legal?" That was the first order of business for him. I wanted him to ask instead, as the first order of business, "Is it moral?" He was not entirely wrong, of course. There's little chance of something good getting off the ground, no matter how moral it is, if it brings the parish into conflict with the civil law—or the insurance firm.

Our lives are governed by two laws. There's the civil law. And there's the moral law. Most times they are in harmony. Sometimes they are in conflict. When a conflict occurs, we must follow the higher moral law. In doing this, we have to be prepared to accept the civil consequences, whatever they may be.

In today's Gospel, Jesus speaks of two laws—that of "the Law and the Prophets" and his own. They are not in conflict with one another, but they are very different in quality from one another. Jesus says that he has not come to destroy the Law and the Prophets but to fulfill it—and to perfect it!

The "Law and the Prophets" is basically the Ten Commandments. We all know them. However, they were often interpreted in a way that Jesus disapproved. The Ten Commandments are all about "righteousness," about standing right with God and with the neighbor. The first three have to do with our right relationship with God; the last seven have to do with our right relationships with the neighbor. The old Law said that we must worship God—and people did.

But Jesus said that we are to worship God in a more excellent way—with a full heart and with every fiber of our being behind the nice words on our lips.

The old Law said that people must give strict justice to the neighbor—"an eye for an eye, a tooth for a tooth"—but Jesus showed us a more excellent way when he said that our justice must not be mathematical but, rather, overflow with compassion and mercy. The old Law said that you must forgive your neighbor once. Those who really excelled in the Law forgave their neighbor three times. Peter, thinking himself extravagantly merciful, suggested "seven times." Our Lord's more excellent way demands "seventy times seven times." In other words, the follower of Jesus forgives as often as the offending neighbor is genuinely sorry.

Jesus calls us to an excellence of moral life that reaches beyond the letter of the Law and the commandments. We shall do the right thing from the very best of motives, and we shall do it with a wide and a generous heart. With Jesus, minimal moral requirement is out: excellence of moral living is in.

79A Seventh Sunday in Ordinary Time

MATTHEW 5:38–48

Be Holy!

Here is Jesus insisting that his followers be perfect as their heavenly Father is perfect! And here are we trying to keep our heads above the rising waters of doubt and unbelief around us! I think that, down deep, we may feel a bit disappointed that Jesus is demanding that we be perfect in an age of chronic imperfection. Should he not be praising us, instead, just for our basic endurance?

Sometimes we feel that we are fighting a rearguard action with the faith. Sometimes we feel that even the official Church is not helping us. For example, the fundamental religious issue of the last century and of this new century is faith in God and the lack of it, belief and unbelief. Here are we priests scrambling on a Saturday afternoon for "a story" or "a few words" that will get us through the homily on Saturday night or Sunday morning. And here is the world engaging our young people—at great length and passionately—with its philosophy of me-ism and greed. And here is Jesus, in the middle of all this unbelief and me-ism, demanding that we become perfect as our heavenly Father is perfect! Is he serious? Indeed, yes.

When God first chose the Jews (the ancient Hebrews), he did so in order to fashion for himself a people different from all the others, and particularly like himself. He told them, "You shall be holy, because I am holy" (Leviticus 11:44). Of you and me, the new people of God, Paul says, "He saved us and called us to a holy life" (2 Timothy 1:9). Saint Peter says, ". . . be holy yourselves in every aspect of your conduct, for it is written, 'Be holy because I (am) holy' " (1 Peter 1:15–16). But you are "a chosen race, a royal priesthood, a holy nation, a people of his own" (1 Peter 2:9).

We are, according to these scriptures, called to holiness, not to just a bare-bones faith and minimal moral practice. And yet, our shepherds seem pleased enough if we can manage to hold on to any faith at all in this generation and time. I am not condemning them. What is killing us, I think, is our politically correct feeling that we should not be too different from anyone else in the world. We do not feel that we should be religiously elitist in a democratic age. What's killing us, too, is that we don't see any great results from our efforts. What's killing us also is the holding pattern, rather than the fearless evangelizing pattern that we think we see in Church leaders today, the pope himself being the lovely exception. What's killing us, most of all, is the pervading influence of the secular that has little place for God and for his Son's priorities and values. In fighting all of this, we also have to fight our own kids' laid-back values and disvalues. It's all a big plate on our table in a time of small spiritual appetite.

Religion, as a process for significant change in our lives and in the life of society, will continue to fail, and it will continue to drag its feet drearily through our own personal lives until we accept scriptures like today's Gospel with a sense of their radical demands. "Be holy, for I your God am holy!" This word of God is intended seriously and radically. All but the saints take it in an accommodated sense. That is our trouble.

This may be the biggest bite of all on our big plate: that we apply the scriptural demands to ourselves, and no longer accommodate them to our ease, or to some soft and, basically, useless interpretation. Remember what the Lord said about the lukewarm? (See Revelation 3:16.)

Ask God for the grace of appreciating the wonder—for it surely is that—of being chosen by Him for holiness in this life.

82A Eighth Sunday in Ordinary Time

MATTHEW 6:24–34

Trusting in Providence

Jesus, in this Gospel, is still addressing last week's Gospel topic: the Christian's vocation to holiness. What is holiness?—being a believer who trusts God absolutely and who becomes "whole" or complete in the likeness of God.

We cannot become holy, and we do not trust God, if we try to serve the Lord with the god of material concern and the god of worry already enthroned in our hearts.

Our Lord is not condemning material possessions as such. All of us must have some if we are not to become welfare wards of the government. Our Lord is condemning the inhumanness—for that is what it is—of "the material girl" and "the material boy." Such is the person who idolizes money and material possessions, who lives by a philosophy of "things," and who would trample on others for the sake of having more things. Where is God in that picture? He's dead on the sidelines.

Nor is the Lord condemning normal worry when we mean, by that, prudent concern in our affairs. But some people worry so much that they are a strain on everyone else around them. And their relationship with God becomes strained too. Worry disrupts healthy religion.

Our Lord is making a fundamental contrast, in this Gospel, between the priorities of the secular world and the priorities of the faith. He says in effect, Don't live as pagans live: live as believers who trust God's providence must live. We may recall that the original meaning of the word *pagans* is "the people who do not know God."

The key teaching in today's Gospel is this: Follow God's rule for living as your priority; then the money and possessions and things will fit into their proper place in your life. The danger in prioritizing material things is that they become more important than God and people. I saw a bumper sticker one time that spells out the philosophy of the material girl and the material boy: "He [or she] who dies with the most toys wins."

Are we flirting too much with possessions and "things"? Much of the nation has the material psychology that many of our forebears criticized in the wealthy landowners of the great colonial estates and later in the captains and the kings of coal and steel and oil, of industry and commerce. You and I are infiltrated by a nineteenth-century understanding of the American Dream as the promise of making it big in terms of bucks with all the influence and the comfort that the big bucks can buy. But this was not exactly the meaning of the American Dream to our forebears, nor to the drafters of the Declaration of Independence.

Now I'm not condemning money or material possessions and things as such because the Lord didn't. I'm calling for balance when it comes to such things as possessions and worry, and for the proper priorities in our lives, as Jesus did. Am I wrong in saying that all too many in our land define themselves more by what they have than by who they are? H. G. Wells wittingly observed, "You can't have money like that and not swell out" (Kipps, bk. 2). In the bad sense! And in the wrong direction!

The road we should be on is the road of the Gospel of Jesus. The road that is made of money and material possessions and things is a poor road for the human spirit. In the language of the engineers, it's the soft-bottomed road instead of the metalled road. When the rains come, the rains of life that are deep personal tragedy and major human loss, the soft road will not support us. It will only wash away under the stress. Why do so many prioritize the wrong road as their primary road through life? Trust God and his Word instead. Listen to Jesus: "Seek first the kingdom of God and his rule over you, and all these other things will be added to you besides."

85A Ninth Sunday in Ordinary Time

MATTHEW 7:21–27

Christian Sincerity

The trial of war criminals is a study in the way people react to others' condemnation of them. Nearly all war criminals view themselves as innocent of all the charges. (Albert Speer was the sole exception at Nuremberg, though.) They see themselves as people who, to the contrary, should be commended for their patriotism, for their loyalty, for their dedication to the state, and for their devotion to duty and to the institution they swore to serve. Simple humanity is never on their list.

It seems that all of them lose their heads (and their hearts) when devotion to some institution, to some ideology, or to some cause becomes more important to them than people. It is something we have to guard against; because nothing is easier than for one to identify almost exclusively with the institution one spends one's life serving. Some people, even in the Church, glory in that identification. But it is Jesus we must serve, and others (including the Church) only in his name, and never as his replacement. It is crucial for us to remember that people come before institutions, even before earthly holy institutions.

That's the sense I have when I read this sobering Gospel from Jesus. "But Lord, I preached in your name; I worked miracles in your name; I promoted the Church and the Bible in your name;

I spent my life in your work!" For all that, will he say to me on the day of reckoning, "Away from me . . . I do not even know you"?

What he says to me on that day depends greatly, I believe, on my dedication to him, and on what I allow him to do for others through the willing instrument that I am. "He must increase; I must decrease" (John 3:30).

The context of this Gospel passage is our Lord's earlier condemnation of the false prophets of the Old Testament in verse 15. Our Lord points to false New Testament prophets who will come in the future and in his name, after his Ascension. They are false in the sense that all false prophets basically preach themselves. We find several references to these false Christian prophets in the later New Testament writings. Clearly, they plagued the early Church as false prophets had once plagued Israel, and as false prophets infect every generation, including our own.

As with Old Testament prophets, so with Christian prophets: we must judge them by the growth of God and grace that they effect in people's hearts. All the spectacular stuff means nothing if it fails that one, critical yardstick.

Biblical scholar John P. Meier says that Jesus, in this passage, is threatening "showy but empty Christians" with a severe judgment, and he notes that "the church and especially her flashy leaders" are not exempt. He adds that Matthew wishes to include "all sorts of charismatic wonder-workers" in the Church of Matthew's own time. They were the ones who were stealing Matthew's thunder!

You and I are not false prophets or dazzling wonder-workers, so how shall we relate the Lord's words to ourselves? Perhaps the benchmark for us is just the simple matter of our sheer sincerity in all that we do for Jesus and for others in his name. We promote him and not ourselves. He must always increase; we must always decrease.

88A Tenth Sunday in Ordinary Time

MATTHEW 9:9–13

Hypocrites and Hospitals

Today's Gospel can be the springboard for addressing two issues. The first is the charge that the Church is full of hypocrites. The other is the perennial tendency of the preferred and pampered layer of society to look down its nose on others who are on the bottom rungs of the social and economic ladder.

Hypocrisy is professing one thing and practicing its opposite. It is a deliberate thing. I have every reason to believe that most people in the Church are doing the best they can. Their sins result from their weaknesses, not from malice or pretense. They are not hypocrites: they are sinners. We all are, to some degree. Therefore, the Church is not full of hypocrites: it is full of sinners.

A pastoral weakness of the moment is our loss of the sense of sin and, so, of the need of redemption. This may explain why so many are no longer at church, and why those of us who still are may be tempted sometimes to wonder why; especially the young. But we *are* sinners. And so, the Church is full of sinners. It should be. It is their hospital. "Those who are well do not need a physician, but the sick do. Go and learn the meaning of the words, 'I desire mercy, not sacrifice.' I did not come to call the righteous but sinners" (Matthew 9:13).

In the Gospel, the Pharisees take issue with the Lord for eating with sinners. The Pharisees are not exactly the righteous of the Bible who can look God in the eye. They are self-righteous, an entirely different category—and a sinful one. Perhaps they, more than anyone else, are truly sinners. But they do not see themselves as sinners. On the contrary, they see themselves as the dutiful upholders and interpreters of God's law and Jesus as a misinterpreter of it. As a misinterpreter, the Lord is a threat not only to the Pharisees but to society. They never lose their suspicion in his regard, nor their opposition

to him. As the Hebrew root of their name indicates, they see themselves as the "separated" ones, a class apart from everyone else. Their
great sin is their pride.

Religious people today can be self-righteous after the manner
of the Pharisees. They can be so self-satisfied that they see no need
of anyone's help for themselves. It is a temptation that maybe bishops
and priests and ministers and catechists are prone to. One can become
so used to supervising and teaching and confessing others that one
is almost immune to the incoming challenge of the word of God for
oneself, and to self-confession as a sinner.

The sophistication of the Western world has elements of the
Pharisaic about it too. It is self-sufficient. It doesn't really need God
anymore. And it is elitist. Despite its democratic and egalitarian roots,
it looks down its nose on the poor and on the plain, and on the strug-
gling layers of humanity that the Bible might call the "people of the
land." The Hebrew "people of the land" were, historically, the agricul-
tural illiterates, the farmers and the shepherds, who were caught up
in dirt and dung all day long, and so were unable to be ritually clean.
How the Pharisees despised them!

Today, perhaps, the "people of the land" ("the country people"
in the Jerusalem Bible translation) are judged by the elitists to be not
only the hicks and the hillbillies of the mountains, but also the urban
poor, assorted drifters and bag people, the asylum seekers and the
migrant workers who lack up-market suavity, who would not know
whether Chardonnay is a wine or a town, and whose piety might be
better reflected in the songs of Nashville than on the pages of Vatican II.

Elitist discrimination can be a first step to other things.
Name-calling and the categorization of others, even if done only in
the privacy of one's heart, is unchristian. Is the elitism of our time,
be it social or religious, and despite trailing its own clouds of question
marks, weaknesses and sin, rushing to arrive at the summit with
the Pharisees?

We are sinners. Let us acknowledge that. And we need Jesus.
He came to call us. The self-righteous are sinners, too, and they need
the Lord perhaps more than we ourselves do. Let us pray for them,
even as we pray for ourselves.

91A Eleventh Sunday in Ordinary Time

MATTHEW 9:36—10:8

Harvesting

Each of us sees things differently. A group of us could stand on a piece of high ground in the middle of a prairie and someone might ask us later, "What did you see?" One of us might say, "I saw a big empty space." Someone else might say, "I saw what the plains looked like a long time ago." Another might say, "I saw development potential and maybe a city there some day." Still another might say, "To be honest, I didn't see much; I was wondering if there was oil there."

We see people differently too. The Gospel tells us that Jesus saw the crowds lying prostrate with exhaustion and he had pity on them, for they were like sheep without a shepherd. William Barclay says that, by way of contrast, the orthodox religious leaders in Jesus' time would have looked on the same crowds with disdain. "The Pharisees saw the common people as chaff to be destroyed and burned up" (William Barclay, *Matthew*). Biblical scholar John P. Meier, in his Matthew commentary, makes much the same observation: "Matthew stresses the sense of compassion Jesus feels for the crowds of ordinary Jews, dejected because they lack true leaders. They look like frightened sheep who simply fall helpless and exhausted to the ground" (John P. Meier, *Matthew*).

What Jesus sees and has compassion on—the people—moves him to speak of the harvest and the need of laborers to gather in the harvest, or as we used to say, he speaks of mission and men. The harvest, dear friends, is great. The harvest is the people of every place and time who must be given the opportunity of hearing the Good News of salvation and the opportunity of being gathered into the kingdom of God. The harvest needs many laborers and Jesus cannot gather the harvest without them. In this Gospel passage, he mentions the harvest and the need of harvesters in the same breath. The one will not be gathered in without the other, for Jesus cannot do it all alone.

There is a parallel here to that other scene in which Jesus is likewise moved to compassion by a huge number of people and by their helpless condition. The scene is the feeding of the "five thousand, not counting women and children." (See Matthew 14:13–21.) These people had left their homes, gone out to "a deserted place" where Jesus was, and spent the whole day listening to him. As the sun began to set they were far from home, had nothing to eat, and were very hungry. There, too, Jesus involved others—his disciples—in what he was doing: in feeding the multitude.

It seems to me that the harvest is great in every generation. Maybe equally, the laborers are less than sufficient. Is that why Jesus tells us to pray for more harvesters, knowing that his words would apply to a greater or lesser degree in every generation of the Church's history? Who are the harvesters? To put it in a nutshell, the harvesters are all of us!

The harvest that Jesus speaks of, the harvest that must be gathered, is the whole human world. It must be invited to his Gospel and to his grace. I believe that bishops, priests, and deacons will remain indispensable laborers in this and in all the generations. I ask your support of them through your prayers and your love, through your word of encouragement and your word of gratitude. And I ask you also to listen to the compassionate Lord's admonition—because he did not make it in an off-handed manner—that we "beg the harvest master (that is, God) to send out laborers to gather the harvest." Our Lord is asking here for prayers that come from the deepest part of us. If such be the quality of our prayers, then the Church and the harvest will be gifted with many and good priestly vocations and dedicated workers for the Lord.

We need to pray for other harvest laborers too. We need to pray for harvesters in the laity—yourselves! The work of the harvest is too vast to be fulfilled by the clergy alone. The "domestic church," the church of the home, needs its Christian parental shepherds also as never before. The Church in the community needs its Christian witnesses of faith and love. The harvest field of the modern marketplace of commerce, communications, and ideologies needs more Christian men and women who are the Gospel-in-the-flesh that challenges the marketplace's "this-world-only" focus and values.

We are all called to be laborers for the Lord of the harvest in one way or another. The harvest needs its priestly and its lay vocations. The Second Vatican Council reminds us of that truth. The Church is of its very nature missionary, and all of us without exception are the Church and are its missionaries.

Let us pray, then, for many and good vocations to the priesthood, and for many and good vocations to the lay apostolate in its many forms today.

94A Twelfth Sunday in Ordinary Time

MATTHEW 10:26–33

The Courage of Our Convictions

During the first visit of Pope John Paul II to Los Angeles, a number of years ago, all pastors including me were required to line the streets with our parishioners. My people and I took our appointed place, and we were immediately confronted by fundamentalist Christian preachers. They moved through our ranks with amplified voices, urging us to see the light, to come out from the abomination of Rome, and to come under the saving blood of Jesus.

I was upset. They lacked good manners. They were raining on our parade. Our school children were confused. It was still the time when I knew best in their eyes, and here was a preacher shouting repentance through a megaphone into my ear. An adult parishioner saw my anger and said, "Well, you have to admit that we Catholics wouldn't have the guts to stand up like that, and risk being jailed for Jesus." I grant that the parishioner was probably right.

All sorts of others turned out for the pope's visit, too. It was the ideal public platform for everyone, from aggressive Catholic feminists to gays dressed up as nuns, to vent their anger and steal a slice of the TV coverage. And they did.

I think that we ordinary Catholics are, by comparison, a tame lot. I think we are the last ones on the planet—with a few exceptions— who would think of getting out there in public and mucking into people and issues for the sake of Christ. Why is that?

One or two factors come to mind. I think that the laity have been psychologized into letting the clergy speak for them. And I think that the laity, generally speaking, do not have the adult religious education and the adult spiritual formation that make other Christians fearless for Christ. There are exceptions, of course, but exceptions only prove the general rule. I think our laity have never been trained to discern the voice of the Spirit speaking to them in the marketplace, urging them on for Christ. And I think that the virtue of spiritual courage has contracted in all of us under pressure of the recent scandals, the cautious faith, and the comfortable materialism.

And yet, here is Jesus with full-blown confidence in his followers: "What you hear whispered, proclaim on the mountain tops!" Spread the mysteries of the kingdom of God that have been hidden until now! Until you and me! Make disciples of all peoples without exception! Spread the good news! Spread the grace! Spread the faith! Spread the fire!

The Western world has long been slipping into infidelity, and now our own society is in danger of it. *Infidelity* is a word more properly connected with unfaithfulness to God than with unfaithfulness to one's spouse. *Infidelity* for believers is not the sin of abandoning God totally, or of heresy. It is the sin of silence—silence about God and silence with his word. We have become such a silent Church! We are mostly absent from present-day social dialogue and seem to have little effect on the great national debates. What little we do seems to be done more and more in secret as if we were afraid to speak boldly for Christ and for his Church's values, and to be known and named as bold messengers.

"Fear no one," says Jesus in the first line of today's Gospel. Sometimes I look at our cardinals and bishops, at our priests and people and at myself, and wonder where we stand. Then I look at a certain man in Rome—who may not embody everyone's theology or hopes or pastoral priorities—but for whom I lined my Los Angeles street those many years ago, and put my school children into the shock of anti-Catholic megaphones. The pope is still doing, with age and Parkinson's, what he did then, full of a youthful vigor. He still holds up the Lord Jesus before the world's face. It is his way of saying to all about him and to all out there in TV land, "This is your Savior! You have no other in this world, and you and your society are slipping away from him!"

This now fragile pope is still full of human courage, and even of Christ's fearlessness. He is still full of Gospel proclamation. He is still an example to all of us.

Jesus said, "What I say to you in the darkness, speak in the light; what you hear whispered, proclaim on the housetops."

97A Thirteenth Sunday in Ordinary Time

MATTHEW 10:37–42

Interlinked

We have buses and trains that claim to be our "interlink." It's a nifty slogan that signals convenient connections for the traveling public. If you do a little financial investing, you are likely to know something about interlinked funds. Various groups around the world, who have similar interests, practice another form of interlinking. It is called networking. Linkage is the name of their game too.

Today's Gospel passage is about linkage. Jesus mentions the four who are interlinked in the work of salvation. They are the Father, himself, the apostle, and the disciple-learner. The Father sends the Son with his message of love and salvation. The Son carries the Father's message to the apostle. The apostle gives the message to the disciple-learner. All of them accept the Father's message and put it into practice. And all of them receive the Father's reward, which is gratitude now and eventual glory with Him in heaven. All are linked in what is called the divine plan of salvation.

All of this is very nice. There's a fine flow to it, and a logical interlinkage. But it is hard for some Christian disciples to see themselves, easily and gracefully, interlinked in this plan. I have in mind especially the ones whose lives are full of pain and of long-term suffering. There is such a long-term sufferer in my own family. And, of course, I've known others.

Other examples? I have the memorial card of a Father Donal Mary Gearty. He was a seminarian with me. He died, the card says, "in the fifth year of his ministry." He died of cancer. The Lord took him in a shorter time than it took for the seminary to train and ordain him. There was a Father Michael O'Sullivan who went to the West Coast from the Midwest, and spent the short years of his priesthood on his back in a sanatorium. The number of liturgies he celebrated, with vestments on, could be counted by the dozens, not by the thousands.

Where does this kind of serious suffering fit into the linkage of the divine plan? Chronic suffering goes against the grain of our humanity. We live with the increasing expectation that sooner or later, and increasingly sooner, medical technology will give us all the answers and defeat all this serious suffering. Even theology urges us, more nowadays than in the past, to seek our answers in medicine and to attribute less of our suffering to the will of God. In hospital visits, we priests strain our theology at times as we alternate our message to our suffering parishioners between hope in the medical team and surrender to God's inscrutable will. We do not know ourselves how to name their suffering lest we undermine their ray of hope, on the one hand, or their surrender in trusting faith, on the other.

Part of the word that Jesus passed on to us is what to do with suffering, and what to do with that ultimate level of suffering which is death. We learn much from Jesus. He did not willingly look for suffering or death himself. But when he realized that they had to be endured, for the Father's glory and our salvation, he surrendered; but only then. Why else was he on the mountain talking to Moses and Elijah before he "set his face like flint" for Calvary? (See Isaiah 50:7.) Why else would he say in his agony, "My Father, if it is possible, let this cup pass from me" (Matthew 26:39).

All of us, quite understandably, want to be disciples and messengers in a spectacular way rather than in a suffering way. We want the gifts and the charisms, the splendid offices and the wonderful tongues of the divine interlinkage. We would rather avoid Saint Paul's instruction that we are "always carrying about in the body the dying of Jesus" (2 Corinthians 4:10). We identify easily with the healing and the spectacular Christ, but much more fearfully with the suffering and the broken Christ.

When suffering cannot be avoided, we may curse it or claim it with a surrendering faith. The disciple-learner claims it. If we claim it with faith, we will receive a matching pattern from the life of Christ for our own lives, and an amazing personal grace. We will come to know that the power of God is as operative in the Via Dolorosa as it is on the Damascus road. We will tell ourselves—it is really the Spirit telling us—that if there is a human source from which the Church draws its spectacular gifts and charisms of grace, that source is the martyrs and the believers whose long-term pain and suffering builds up what is lacking to the sufferings of Christ in his body that we call the Church.

Take the light of a candle. It is a tip of white light growing from its base of purple flame. Some in the Church, with their gifts and their offices, are the tip of white light. Others, with the offering of their pain, are the crucible foundation. The divine plan of salvation is always a tip of white light building from a stem of purple fire. We must tell those who are suffering grievously that the work of salvation is always a passage through fire for some, so that others may be wonder and light in the world in order to save it.

100A Fourteenth Sunday in Ordinary Time

MATTHEW 11:25–30

Can We Know God Today?

All of us can be jealous little creatures. There's nothing startling in that. We are familiar with jealousy among professionals in the same line of work, and even in the same office. Inter-service rivalry in the military has sometimes put the outcome of a critical battle in doubt. It's tough enough to do battle with your enemy without having to do battle with the jealousy of your fellow patriots as well!

One time I lived in a large rectory while doing special ministry. My fellow priests in the rectory were the parish priests. My work was with the archdiocese. They loved to rib me: "You special ministry guys think you're great intellectuals, but your heads are up in the clouds. On the other hand, we parish men are the practical guys with all the common sense."

One morning, on my way to the chancery, I noticed that the parish church looked different on the outside. I stopped my car and looked at the building. I admit it took me more than a few seconds to spot what was missing. All the old, expensive copper drain pipes were gone! Thieves had come in the night and cut them as far up as their ladders took them. I phoned the local police department and then continued to the office. I can tell you that the guys with all the common sense were shocked when a patrol car arrived at their door some time later, asking about missing pipes.

We still have clergy and seminarians who like to quote Jesus in today's Gospel about the mysteries of God being hidden from the learned but revealed to the simple—read: hidden from the supposedly intelligent but revealed to the supposedly less intelligent. They use it as an excuse for not cracking open a few books a month and keeping up with their studies. We must learn again that intelligence is not a threat to the Church, as Augustine and Aquinas so ably demonstrate, but that the clerical put-down of intelligence raises a question about the integrity of our Church for all thinking men and women. The Gospel is for all humankind, not just for the pious and the safe and the simple.

Our Lord is not offering any of us an excuse for intellectual laziness through this Gospel today—or for theological ignorance; or for the stifling of prophecy. Nor is he offering the laity an excuse for ignorance of their faith. He is, I believe, illustrating the truth that our faith in him requires total trust, such as an infant has in its mother, and that it is to these trusting, whole-hearted believers—intelligent or less so—that he reveals what he has from his Father.

Our Lord makes a startling claim in this Gospel. No one knows the Father except the Son, and those to whom the Son chooses to reveal Him. People today, especially the young, say that God is unknowable, that He is too distant, that He is too vague. God has become a kind of vague, indefinite aura beyond the clouds, or at the tail end of the modern consciousness. No one knows what God is really like, people say. So how can you possibly have a relationship with the inscrutable? This vague God is the cause of our agnosticism and of our religious indifference. So the complaint goes.

And here is Jesus, responding to all of that in today's Gospel. In effect, he is saying, "I know God. I reveal God to you. Look at me, and you look at God. Look into my face, and you are looking into the face of God. Know what I'm like, and you will know everything worthwhile about God." Philip said to Jesus one time, "Master, show us the Father and that will be enough for us." And Jesus answered, "Whoever has seen me has seen the Father" (John 14:8–9).

It is time for all of us, especially young people, to open the Gospels and to do some serious walking through its pages in the company of Jesus. He reveals—so persuasively—the "unknowable" God to us.

103A Fifteenth Sunday in Ordinary Time

MATTHEW 13:1–23 (LONGER) OR MATTHEW 13:1–9 (SHORTER)

Words, Words, Words!

The seed that Jesus sowed is the word of God. Our world turns on words. We need them to communicate with each other. Words come in many shapes. All of our constitutions and our charters are set in words. All our codes of law are written in words. So are our sacred books. Even the flashing images on our TV screens are transpositions of pages of words that someone wrote in a script.

The Bible tells us that God has spoken many words in our world. Everything good in the universe is a word that God spoke. Since God's word is always spirit and life, His spoken words become realities around us. The marvels of nature, the processes of life, the whirling constellations are His words. The poet Joseph Mary Plunkett wrote: "[Even] rocks are His written words" *(I See His Blood upon the Rose)*.

There is a very special word among the many words God has spoken. It is a *unique* word. We hear it at the liturgy every Sunday. This particular word of God is the one kind of word that really matters. Why? Because of all the words that serve us, only one can save us. That word is "The word of the Lord."

What is the saving word? It is the Word of God that became flesh and lived among us. This word is a person. It is Jesus of Nazareth. He speaks to every generation. He speaks to us. Are we listening? "The word of the Lord." "The gospel of the Lord." Do we take his word in? Do we grow with his word?

Jesus explained the story about the sower and the seed. He himself is the sower. The seed is his word. We are the soil that receives the word. There are different kinds of soil, and his word gets different receptions among us. Some of us are hard, compacted soil that his word cannot penetrate. Our minds and hearts are shut. The usual form of the shut mind and heart is prejudice. I am sure you have all met people who just don't want to hear about God, or about the demands of his word on them.

Some of us are the rocky soil. Rocky soil is shallow ground; too much stone, too little soil. Some of us, in the modern frenetic age, are what T. S. Eliot called "the hollow men" *(The Hollow Men)*. We live by passing fads and momentary intensities. We take to Jesus like we take to the latest car model, all enthusiasm at first, and outgrow him within a year or two. Or we get religious at a mission in Lent—and the fervor is dead by Easter.

Some of us are the thorny ground. We are soil that is full of thorns and thistles and scrub. Our minds and hearts are crowded with cares and committees, even with too many works of charity. Our life is so packed. We make quality time for everyone except for the word of God speaking to us. Pope Pius XII once called this the heresy of activity. God is in this picture, of course, but as someone has said he's in the picture "as second best, and second best is always the worst enemy of best" (William Barclay, *Matthew*).

Some of us are the good soil. Our minds and hearts are open, and they receive the word and put it into action. We yield results, ten- or thirty- or a hundred-fold, depending on our heart and our individual commitment to the word of the Lord.

We must treasure the Lord's saving word above all other words in our lives. It is the only word that saves us. We must commit ourselves to growing day by day with the word, even to the fullest measure possible. For the fast-passing years tell us that time is limited; and they tell us very soberly that, with the passing years, so pass away all the human words, and all the novelties and all the intensities, without which we thought we could not live. Only the word of the Lord "remains forever" (1 Peter 1:25).

106A Sixteenth Sunday in Ordinary Time

MATTHEW 13:24–43 (LONGER) OR
MATTHEW 13:24–30 (SHORTER)

An Enemy Has Done This

We tend to think of the enemy as someone outside the family, outside the Church. But you are, I'm sure, familiar with the wisdom of these anonymous words: "We searched for the faces of our enemies, and found them in our own."

Jesus, one time, said as much: ". . . and one's enemies will be those of his household" (Matthew 10:36). There was Judas, who was "one of his company." There was Peter who "denied him three times." There was John the beloved, who watched the suffering of Christ "from a distance."

In the case of the Church, a lot of the enemies are within. There was the priest Arius who led many into believing that Christ had only one nature, and Archbishop Nestorius who made others believe that Christ was two persons. Much later, the Church was split East–West during the Great Schism, and North–South at the Protestant Reformation. Whether these men or Rome itself caused most of the damage is of little interest here. The point is that the enemies who ravage the Church are as much within as without. And what of our own time, and the dismal moral decade we have just left behind us? Our recent enemies have been ourselves.

There will always be weeds among the wheat in the Church. And there usually is a weed or two in the Christian lives of the best of us. Our Lord is not suggesting that we let our own weeds bloom! He is pointing up a reality in the life of all institutions, and a reality in the Church's own life. And he is not pointing to it with joy.

If we are not to be disheartened by sin and scandal in the Church, then we must know that they will be present at all times, as the weeds are present among the wheat. Wheat and weed will continue to grow side by side in the field that is the Church. At the harvest time, that is, at the judgment, the weeds will be burned and the wheat filled into God's granary.

This is a cautionary tale, from the Lord himself, to all of us who are the Church. The tale has its parallels in all institutions, and its social parallel in the nation's spy cases, insider securities trading, bribery, and sundry court cases. The caution is this: People are not always as they seem, whether in society or in the Church. One's bishop or religious superior may turn out to be one's major spiritual disappointment in life. One's priest may turn out to be the predator of one's children. One's visionary may turn out to be a sham; one's faith healer, a quack.

While the good Lord is teaching us to be guarded in our loyalties and in our enthusiasms, he is also telling us not to make easy judgments before the time when he will do the judging, the time of ultimate disclosure. The Church is a location for easy gossip and rumor-mongering. They ill-befit believers and they are a form of forbidden judgment before the time. They disturb faith and charity. They upset those who are the butt of rumors, and they distract each of us from concentrating on the Lord and from personal spiritual growth.

Realistically, I have found in my own lifetime that I have no enemies worthy of the name. I have only the hurt of a few failed friends. And I am conscious that I, in my turn, am the hurt of a failed friend to others both known and unknown. So, these days, I look more and more into the mirror at myself in the mornings. I suppose it's because I'm getting older by the day and I am watching for the lines that count the passing of my years. I see only one face looking back at me every morning from the mirror. And I say to it, "If I have any enemy at all that could do me real harm, it is you, my closest friend." I say it seriously because, at this stage of my life, only I can spiritually harm me, and I have no desire to be among the weeds on the last day.

109A Seventeenth Sunday in Ordinary Time

Matthew 13:44–52 (longer) or Matthew 13:44–46 (shorter)

A Gilt-Edged Investment

Usually the best and the tallest buildings in any city are the banks and insurance and investment houses. They proudly advertise their goal, which is to get you to invest your money with them so they, in turn, can invest it somewhere else. And what is your money but the years of your life measured in time, toil, and sweat. This investment invests you!

Our Lord wants us to invest ourselves in the kingdom of God. I think that if he were speaking today instead of two thousand years ago, he would not use the words *treasure* and *pearl* for the kingdom of God, but some modern words such as *high-yield deposit* and *gilt-edged investment*. Being part of the fellowship of the kingdom now, and being part of the effort to spread it, is a gilt-edged investment for our future in heaven.

William Barclay says that the image of the man finding treasure in a field is very apt for our Lord's time. People did not have banks then as we know banks today. But they did have banks! They did not put their large coins and their gold ornaments into buildings but into an earthen pot in the ground. These pots were common. Do you remember the parable of the talents, and the servant who did not invest his master's money but "buried it"? He put it in a pot in the ground for safe keeping! He was too afraid to invest it.

Sometimes, people died and left unclaimed pots after them. The whereabouts of some of these pots faded with the passing of the years. That is why treasure hunting was quite common in the Lord's time. Under Jewish rabbinical law, the finder of the treasure was entitled to keep it, whether it was a great or a small trove. In fact, the phrase "finders keepers" probably originates with this Jewish rabbinical law since an almost identical Hebrew phrase is written there.

The emphasis in the story in the Gospel is on the sheer joy of the man who found the pot of treasure. Our Lord is telling us that we should be ecstatic over finding our place in the kingdom of God. Like the man in the story, we should be willing to sell all, give up everything, if need be, for this kingdom. It is the pearl beyond all price.

There are many pearls in our lives. These are our spouse, our children, our girl- or boyfriend, our country, our landscape, our books, our music, our sports, and even our fine wines! Our Lord is not denying us any of these. He is simply putting our graced life in him at the center of the string of pearls. It is the pearl above all pearls.

The kingdom of God is the incalculable find, the priceless pearl, our gilt-edged investment. It is not everyone's. But, through God's mysterious grace, it is yours and it is mine. Why is it ours and not others'? This side of heaven we will never really know. We have to rely on Saint Paul's magnificent but mysterious explanation in the second reading of today's Mass for a glimpse of an answer. Paul writes: "For those he foreknew he also predestined to be conformed to the image of his Son, so that he might be the firstborn among many brothers. And those he predestined he also called; and those he called he also justified; and those he justified he also glorified" (Romans 8:29–30).

Paul is describing you and me in the kingdom of God. Let our whole lives be confidently and gratefully invested in it!

112A Eighteenth Sunday in Ordinary Time

MATTHEW 14:13–21

Christ's Compassion

Carlo Carretto, in *Letters from the Desert*, said that in the face of a third of the world menaced by starvation, he could no longer enjoy economic stability. So he packed his bag, went off to the Sahara desert, became a hermit, and earned his living cutting up old tires to make "indestructible" sandals for the Tauregs and tourists of the desert.

Carretto felt that it would be good for all of us to put ourselves "every now and then in the condition of having to say, 'Give us this day our daily bread,' with real anxiety because the larder is empty."

The crowds in today's Gospel, who followed Jesus out into the desert, put themselves in that position. By evening they were very hungry, and our Lord's disciples were becoming alarmed. They urged him to send the people away to the nearest towns and villages. Jesus said, ". . . give them some food yourselves." If the disciples had had enough faith, I have no doubt that the power of Christ would have entered them and they would have been able to feed the people. But, perhaps, fear of a riot or of a tragedy was in their hearts; compassion was in our Lord's heart.

We notice that five thousand men were fed, not counting the women and the children. Despite the numbers, there were twelve basketfuls left over. They symbolize the abundance of Christ's compassion for people.

We also notice that the Lord includes the disciples in the distribution of the food that he has made available. This symbolizes his desire that we become the hands of God's giving to others.

There is the intimation, too, in this feeding episode of the Eucharist yet to come. Matthew describes Jesus by liturgical gestures— he took the bread, looked up to heaven, blessed it, broke it, gave it to them. Matthew sees a type of the future Eucharist in this episode at the start of the Lord's ministry. He is allowed to do so because, in the Christian estimation, bread was always intended to reach its higher function as food for the soul.

You and I, in the face of a third of the world menaced by starvation, need to say our blessing before and after meals with real meaning. You and I, in the face of selfishness and prejudice, need to become the compassion of Christ to others. You and I, in the face of numbing habit, need to approach the gift of the Eucharist again with the eyes of a first-communion child.

115A Nineteenth Sunday in Ordinary Time

MATTHEW 14:22–33

Stormy Weather

Have you ever wondered why democratic governments have public assembly laws that are restrictive? We understand why dictators and totalitarian regimes have such laws, but why the democracies? Citizens have the civil rights of association and of public assembly, yet these are limited by the law and by the police. Governments have a good reason for controlling and limiting the size of crowds: they can easily get out of hand and become a danger to all of us.

There are a number of times in the life of Jesus when the crowd around him is about to get out of hand, and it seems that such a moment is present in today's Gospel. The crowd is large, and their fervor is high. Perhaps the crowd is about to try once again to make Jesus their king—their *political* ruler. That is something he does not want. Perhaps the apostles are caught up in this fervor, too. And perhaps that is why Jesus, to use the Gospel's own word, *made* the apostles get into the boat and head across the water to the other side. Then, alone, he is able to calm the crowd.

A little later, he is involved in another calming incident. This time, it's the calming of the raging waves that spill over the apostles' boat and threaten to engulf it.

Whether we look at the calming of the crowd or the calming of the waves, the point of the Gospel story is clear: Jesus enters all of our life situations and responds appropriately, whatever our need of the moment is.

On our part, there is only one requirement. It is trust and confidence in the Lord. That is the lesson we learn from Peter's and the apostles' lack of trust. They are in the boat when a squall breaks over the lake. It is a small boat, and it begins to ship water. They become terrified. And yet, they have just witnessed the power of Jesus when he fed "five thousand men, not counting women and children" (Matthew 14:21). If he could make enough bread appear for such a multitude, why should the apostles doubt that he could make waves disappear for a handful of men in a small boat on a relatively small lake?

Even after the calming of the waves, Peter wavers. "Lord, if it is you, command me to come to you on the water," he says. Our Lord says, "Come." But Peter begins to sink. He cries out, "Lord, save me!" Now, notice the words used in the Gospel. Jesus *immediately* responds. He *reaches out* his hand, and grasps Peter. Our Lord does not react as you and I might react toward our distrusting children and friends. We might say, Let them wait a bit! That will teach them not to doubt me! Let them grasp *my* hand first!

Saint Brendan the Navigator had a lovely prayer: "Help me, O God, for my boat is so small and your sea is so great." I am like a small boat tossed about by the storms of life. The little boat of my life is often beset by the threatening waves of temptation and failure, of stress and anxiety. Sometimes I feel I may not even get to the shore of tomorrow, never mind the shore of heaven. I am tempted to give up the ship, to lose courage, and to lose heart. The Lord is saying to me in this Gospel, "Courage, child, do not be afraid! Trust me!" He is saying, "I am present in the storms of your life as much as in the calms of your life. Just put your trust in me at all times."

118A Twentieth Sunday in Ordinary Time

MATTHEW 15:21–28

A Persevering Faith

I think that all of us can identify with the scene in this Gospel. Priests certainly can. The poor haunt the sacristy door where you pass in and out to vest for Mass, or they keep showing up at the rectory door until their persistence pays off. We often give in to them so that the nuisance will go away. As Jesus' disciples said, "Send her away, for she keeps calling out after us."

I've never found a satisfactory way of dealing with the poor, and I know in my heart that most of the money I give the poor serves some useless purpose like indolence or drink. I believe, however, that the time spent with them just may have some undefined value in God's greater plan. I may be fooling myself. At any rate, I'll probably keep at it for whatever length of time is left to me. It is very hard to teach an old dog new tricks.

The woman with a request, in today's Gospel, is a Canaanite. She is non-Jewish. She is a Gentile. Jesus was sent to the house of Israel, not to the Gentiles. In addition, Jews regarded Gentiles as dogs. So, why should Jesus even speak to her? Because of compassion on his part and persistence on hers! That combination ensures that the Lord will grant her request.

You and I may have a question about the Lord's use of the word *dogs*. It is not right, he says, for dogs to eat the children's bread. The children of the household are the Jewish people. Is he, as a Jew following his Jewish religion, calling her a Gentile dog? The scholars point out that there are two words for *dog* in the Greek text of the New Testament. One word is for street dogs; and the other is for lap dogs. One is for the wild ones; the other is for the household pets. Our Lord uses the word for a household pet.

We find in the ministry of Jesus something I like to call the Gospel of the exceptions. These exceptions are the instances where our Lord is "made" to do things that are not in his preplanned agenda. For example, he works his first miracle ahead of schedule at the request of his mother for the young newlyweds who ran out of wine on their great day. In today's Gospel, he chooses to make a Gentile woman part of God's household even though the apostolate to the Gentiles, a task for Paul and the others, is still several years away in the future.

We have here, according to William Barclay, an incident where compassion calls to compassion. The woman is pleading for her daughter, not for herself. Her persistence proves the depth of her compassion for her child. Her persistence is also a grammar of trust and faith. She begins with a social courtesy (first calling Jesus "sir"). Next, she gives him a Jewish messianic title ("Son of David"). Finally, she acknowledges him as "Lord."

If you and I have persistent faith in our Lord, as this Canaanite woman had, then it doesn't matter how impossible our request may seem. The Canaanite woman assures us that our faith and trust will find their appropriate level, and their appropriate response, in the seemingly bottomless well of the Lord's compassion.

121A Twenty-first Sunday in Ordinary Time

MATTHEW 16:13–20

A Servant Church

A few years back, a document was issued from Rome called *Dominus Jesus*. It re-asserts the Catholic Church as the unique church that Jesus founded. It appears to lessen the stature of the other Christian churches. It is a controversial document for many who are involved in the ecumenical dialogue. Such a document would interpret our Gospel today in a way that highlights the Catholic Church as the original church of the Lord's foundation, and the pope as Peter's successor.

I will assume that most of us here have little trouble with all of that. It is, for Catholics, the traditional understanding of this Gospel passage. I would like to balance it, however, with a couple of other considerations so that this Gospel may challenge any smugness we may have about being the true Church, and so that this Gospel may help us in our personal spiritual growth.

There is a time for hiding in the security of the mother's apron, and a time to get out from behind it and face some challenges. I see the Church contracting today in America and in Western Europe. It is getting smaller in numbers (as a proportion of world population) and in influence. It is defensive. It feels oppressed. When an institution is on the defensive, it tends to keep re-asserting its claims on paper instead of engaging in real battle with its real enemies.

One of the real enemies of the Church today is its own failure in adult religious education and formation. Re-asserting the Church's claims to uniqueness alone will not give adult Catholics the tools they need to oppose the errors and salve the "wounds" that *Dominus Jesus* discusses. Some serious parish discussions, and some serious engagement with the word of God, just might.

Why are the mainline Christian churches mostly static today, and why are the small Bible-based ones flourishing? For one thing, the latter are seriously into personal faith and fulfillment through God's word. For another, their leaders and disciples are out there walking the streets and ringing the doorbells, making converts. What of us? When last did you or I make a convert to our faith or bring back a lapsed member? Our Lord is dying, seemingly unnoticed, among us—and not from an active rejection on the people's part but from a kind of allowed indifference on our part. Irish poet and Anglican priest Studdert Kennedy's lines from "The Unutterable Beauty" come to mind:

> When Jesus came to Birmingham, they simply passed him by;
> They never hurt a hair of him, they only let him die.

I notice, in the Gospels, that Jesus does not get into issues of history and apostolic succession in order for a person to decide how the true Church, Jesus' Church, is to be identified. He could scarcely do so, I suppose, since it was all so new at the time. But he must have foreseen the future disunity of Christians, and he could have spelled out some crystal clear markers for identifying his true Church. He didn't—except for one.

And it's the one that keeps getting lost in debates about this church or that church, sister churches or separated churches. It is called the moral argument. It is the one marker that Jesus stressed by which to identify his followers. We cannot ignore it in any discussion about what or where the true Church is. Jesus said, "This is how all will know that you are my disciples, if you have love for one another" (John 13:35). If we were to name the true Church on the basis of this moral argument alone, then the true Church would be the church that best serves the Lord's rule of love. Or it would be the sum of

Christians from all of the churches that love one another. "As I have loved you, so you also should love one another" (John 13:34).

A second thing I notice is that, among the various models of Church that we list today, the saints have invariably favored the servant model. The true Church is the church that is God's servant and the servant of God's people, as the messianic servant, Jesus, uniquely was. It is a Church of servant love. This model of Church is also the one favored by the lowly and the poor, and by the words and actions of Jesus in the Gospels.

We see, in our time, so much of the arrogance that is condemned in the scriptures. Dictators, tyrants, oppressive governments— power-brokers of all kinds—seem to crush people, especially the little ones of the earth. Jesus said it cannot be so with us. The one who is greatest in God's kingdom is the one who is the least of all and the servant of all. We see, in our own land, so much poverty and functional illiteracy, so many broken homes and hearts, so many people abused, ill-used, and victimized. The true Church actively opposes all of this, and is the exemplar of its very opposite. Not on paper, but on the ground!

The Church's drive for respect for life is one that emanates from the model of Church as the servant of the least. The emphasis on the servant model springs also from a deeper spiritual perception of what Gospel and Church really mean. No one in the Church should be interested in displays of power or in the trappings of power—only in the power of the Servant of God, the carpenter's son, the baby born in a stable, the one who had nowhere to lay his head, the divinity that said, "Just so, the Son of Man did not come to be served but to serve and to give his life as a ransom for many" (Matthew 20:28).

If we are the true Church that Jesus set up in today's Gospel, let us prove it to our own time and place, not by paper documents but in abounding servant love.

124A Twenty-second Sunday in Ordinary Time

MATTHEW 16:21–27

Fitting in the Material Things

It is said today that we in the West are the followers of the god of material things. We are big into consumerism of all kinds. I know that the pope criticizes the entire Western world for this. In large measure I agree with him because it undermines the spirit of the Gospel.

I also know that nearly everyone, in nearly every culture, would be quite happy to have their share of this consumerism. Humans have always been consumers, and "things" play a great part in the conduct of a decent human life in this world. Modern material things allow us, in my opinion, the opportunity of a more human lifestyle. They enhance our living environment. They ought to give us a certain freedom and ease and aptitude for a better spiritual life.

Maybe this is one reason why scripture never condemns material things as such. The issue is always whether we elevate them to godly status, and how we use them in our lives. It doesn't profit us anything, in terms of eternal life, if we possess all things and yet lose our souls. The issue in the scriptures is not about condemning material things but about where they should fit properly into our lives.

This morning's Gospel business for us is the challenge of proportionality, that is, fitting things in where they properly should be in our lives. God comes first—then the neighbor. Things must follow them, and only insofar as they enhance our lives. The way of Jesus remains the cross of Jesus. Salvation is found in shouldering our share of the cross, not in drowning in material things.

I once had a part in a play by Kaufman and Hart. It was called *You Can't Take It with You.* Well, we can't take our material things with us, not even one solitary CD. I have a relative who keeps saying, "We're only passing through; we only have the use of things for a while." Even the bumper sticker pagan who says, "He who dies with the most toys wins" knows that all the toys must stay behind, and that the acquisitor's philosophy is an empty one in the final analysis.

I'm sure many of you have looked, with a sad more than a judgmental heart, at the executives who come before our senate or congressional committees and panels and our courts and wondered at their foolishness in the face of pursuing material things. It is sobering to see how the love of money and things has tragically unraveled them in their middle or graying years. How many others are out there—in the flush of youth—who come to grief every year because of the material of life: pop stars, sport stars, economic stars, big fish, and grasping minnows that would be big fish?

What are we to learn from Jesus in today's Gospel? Is it that material things have their place but in their place? Is it that when material things push the cross to the side of our lives, then we have too much of them and too little of the cross? Is it that persons must always come first, God and then neighbor? Or is it that the person who is the least served, and the most reduced, by the mountain of things is my own, spiritually unraveling, materialistic self?

I think it is all of these. Our job, then, is not to set up opposites between material things and spiritual values, but to set priorities. As Jesus said in another place, "But seek first the kingdom [of God] and his righteousness, and all these things will be given you besides" (Matthew 6:33).

127A Twenty-third Sunday in Ordinary Time

MATTHEW 18:15–20

Words for the Lawsuit Culture

We live in a contentious and a litigious age. These are big words which only mean that we like to get in each other's face and take one another to court almost at the drop of a hat. The courts are jammed with our anger and with our real or imagined outrage at our neighbor. We want justice, and we want compensation too! To some degree, the lawyers are responsible for this recourse to the court at the drop of a hat. It's money for them.

But let's not blame the lawyers too much. I think that the crush of population growth and the stress of modern living make us easy targets for getting at our neighbor. It is easy nowadays to feel oppressed, or denied of one's rights, or slighted, or mistreated. A confrontation and compensation psychology is in the air, and it is infiltrating more and more into our Christian hearts.

By way of contrast, we have Jesus in today's Gospel telling Christians that they should settle their differences, not in court but among themselves—face to face, honestly, and with the desire for a peaceful resolution uppermost in their hearts. If the offending party remains stubborn, bring along two or three witnesses and peacemakers. But don't go running to the civil courts. It's not the Christian way of resolving disputes among Christians.

Our Lord could not have said—at this point—"tell the church" (see verse 17), because the Church did not exist then. But it does now. So, should the Church be appealed to for a solution if the offending party remains uncontrite despite the efforts of oneself and of two or three witnesses and peacemakers? The paper answer is yes. And the Church does have a mechanism for resolving disputes among Christians. Realistically, however, genuine Christians will resolve the grievance that divides them through Christ's law of forgiveness and love.

Instead of the contentious and the compensation mentality, we should have the watchman mentality that is mentioned in the first reading today. It is the mentality that both Roosevelt and Churchill brought to their conduct of the Second World War. Both men had a strong sense of being God's watchmen on the walls of democracy and of Christian civilization at a very bad time in history. It was their sense that evil, on the grand scale, had reared its fascist head during their watch and, hence, that they were responsible before God for its destruction and our preservation. We may argue the details of that, but not the deep personal sense that these men had of it. It colors their wartime speeches. Saint Paul puts the watchman mentality another way in the second reading today when he says, "Owe nothing to anyone, except to love one another; for the one who loves another has fulfilled the law" (Romans 13:8).

Each one of us, through our incorporation in Christ, is a watchman on the walls. Who are we watching out for? Not the neighbor to sue him, but the neighbor to love him. Not the neighbor to condemn him, but the neighbor to lift him up. Not society to tear it down by gridlocking the courts, but society to enrich it with our personal wide-heartedness and social responsibility. Not our children to disown them, but our children to lead them.

I am the biblical watchman most of all in my sphere of influence. And that is a relatively small sphere. It is the people within reach of my voice and at my fingertips. It is my spouse, my family, my friends, the people I work with, my immediate neighborhood, and this parish community. These are the few that the Lord has set me to be watchman over, and not the whole wide world. This is the small city on whose walls I watch, in my own time and place.

130A Twenty-fourth Sunday in Ordinary Time

MATTHEW 18:21–35

As Often As

It's been some years now since California passed what was then a very novel drug user law—"three strikes, and you're out." It meant that for the third similar drug use offense you served time in prison. No more excuses. No more pleas. No more bargaining at the bench.

In our Lord's time, there was a similar law regarding offenses by the neighbor against you. You forgave him or her three times. That meant you did not forgive him or her the fourth time, or any subsequent time. Theologian William Barclay tells us in his commentary that this rule was based on the book of Amos. Amos contains a list of sins that God forgives three times. On the fourth, he metes out punishment. It was felt, writes Barclay, that humans should not be more gracious than God, and that forgiveness should be limited to three times only.

Peter is generous. He decides to outdo God and his fellow Jews when he suggests that we forgive our neighbor seven times. Peter must have expected Jesus to applaud his generosity. But Jesus says, "Not seven times, but seventy-seven times." Peter's face must have dropped. How are we to understand seventy times seven times?

Our Lord explains how by means of the story about two servants. One was forgiven a huge debt. Then he turned around and would not forgive his fellow servant the small debt he owed him. God forgives us the huge debt we owe Him for the death of His Son for our sins. So, we must forgive the neighbor, because nothing the neighbor owes us can begin to compare with what we owe God and what He has forgiven us. And the number of the neighbor's offenses against us is insignificant when compared with the bulging number of our ongoing sins that God forgives.

Most of us, I feel, are willing to forgive our neighbor one time. Some of us, twice. A few of us, maybe three times. Then we start drawing a line in the sand. Some of us say, "Three strikes, and you're out!" Is our Lord saying that we must honor our neighbor's repeated sins against us; that we should become a doormat for others' intransigence; and that we must aid and abet their recidivism? I don't believe so. I assume that the Lord is asking us to forgive the person who is truly contrite, and who honestly tries to do better even though that person may offend us again. And that we should keep on forgiving that person if, through weakness, he or she repeats the offense. The *sincere* and *contrite* heart should be forgiven *as often as*.

You have to look at your own heart to see the hearts of others. And you have to read the checkered history of your own life, with a fair measure of empathy and self-forgiveness, to read the checkered lives of others. I know from my own life that people were forgiving of me at various times when they could have, with justification, treated me differently. I believe in the scripture, "Do to others whatever you would have them do to you" (Matthew 7:12). Sometimes that treatment involves our repeated forgiveness of others, just as we have been the beneficiary of others' repeated forgiveness of us.

And if that doesn't motivate you, think of the number of times that a patient God has forgiven you, and will continue to forgive you, *as often as.*

133A Twenty-fifth Sunday in Ordinary Time

MATTHEW 20:1–16A

A Reckless God

The book of Revelation is the last book in the Bible. It is also called the Apocalypse because it has harrowing scenes of destruction when history comes to an end.

For a generation of young Americans, Vietnam was their apocalypse. More bombs were dropped on Vietnam than in all the wars of history combined. Napalm, that fiery mix of jellied gasoline, burned forests and villages and human beings liberally. Nearly every day and night was lit by napalm until the smoking landscape looked as the earth will look at the end, when the seven bowls of God's wrath are poured over it (see Revelation 16).

Wars bring out the best and the worst in human beings, and the Vietnam War was no different. For every heroic act, there was probably a base one to match it. A veteran once told me of a search-and-destroy mission that he was part of. His platoon was ordered to clear suspected Vietcong sympathizers from their village, and then burn it. Some of the platoon were nervous. They were not professional soldiers; they were draftees. Shots were fired. A number of the male civilians fell to the ground. In American eyes, the males were potential Vietcong fighters. One young GI was disgusted by this behavior. He put himself between the civilians and the soldiers, threw down his rifle, and said, "You'll have to kill me first." Somebody did. His death was reported later as an unfortunate accident. All that generous young heart got was a bullet and a free burial back home.

Sometimes we treat God in a similar way. We repay His generosity to us with ingratitude or silence. We look on what we perceive as His greater generosity to others as unfair and, even, unjust. It is as if we wanted to give His great heart the bullet. We are not grateful for the blessings He gives us because others seem to be given more of them. Our judgment on God's heart is the narrow judgment of an eye for an eye and a tooth for a tooth. We would like to reduce His wide heart to the narrowness of our own, rather than widen our hearts to something of the measure of His.

Our Lord asks in the Gospel: "Are you envious because I am generous?" Our standards are always lesser than God's standards. "My thoughts are not your thoughts, and your ways are not my ways," says God in today's first reading. Indeed, the theme of the Mass readings today is the almost reckless generosity of God's heart.

I, personally, have no problem with God's generosity. I delight in it. I am so grateful just to be chosen and called to the vineyard of God, to be part of God's kingdom. It doesn't bother me that others receive more graces than I do. God, not I, is the judge of how much they need and of how much I need. It does not bother me that the last may be first, that late-comers to grace and to salvation may attain sanctity before those of us who have been with the Lord since childhood Baptism, or that they may enjoy a "higher" state in heaven than me.

I do not begrudge God His generosity. I do not question the expanse of His heart. I am grateful that His great heart was there for me in all the ambushes of my life, and that it will be there for me when apocalypse strikes, whether I experience apocalypse as the dramatic ending of the world, or just the customary passage of a human life—my human life—from this world to the next.

136A Twenty-sixth Sunday in Ordinary Time

MATTHEW 21:28–32

Answering an Invitation

We may understand the two sons in today's Gospel in this way.
The second son rejects his father's invitation out of hand. He stands
for the Jewish religious authorities and, through them, for Israel,
God's chosen people. It is to them that Jesus offers the good news
of the kingdom first. They are the children of the promises and,
therefore, the first ones that must be invited into the kingdom by
Jesus. But for the past two chapters in Matthew's Gospel, they have
confronted Jesus with growing opposition and rejection.

The first son stands for the "outsiders," the Gentiles, and all
the others who may have Jewish blood but are blemished in some way.
For instance, the Jewish tax collectors were in the employ of the enemies
of Israel; the Jewish harlots were the enemies of Jewish family life;
the Jewish shepherds and lepers were ritually unclean; the Samaritans
were half-Jewish and heretical; and the Gentiles were in the depth
of theological darkness. There is joy in our Lord's heart that these "outsiders" are accepting his kingdom. But there is sadness as well, because
the religious people are rejecting him.

I'm sure that the acceptance of Jesus by the "outsiders" only
increased the religious opposition to him and so, in a way, put him and
his ministry to Israel in an even worse position.

But there is something more in the parable. The accepting son
is, nevertheless, slow to respond to the father's offer. He must have
mumbled and grumbled a bit before he finally went to work. He does
not express immediate delight in his father's will. Maybe he stands for
us. We are in the kingdom of God, but we are not always delighted
about it. We are not always compliant with God's will. We hesitate
over choices to be made. We grumble a bit. The moral of the story for
us, at any rate, is that we should accept the Gospel with immediate

delight, and respond to it in full obedience. We should neither grumble nor fudge with God's word or God's will or God's kingdom.

If I say that you and I grumble and question the discipline of the Gospel instead of obeying it unquestioningly, I am not suggesting that we should leave our heads behind us when we open the word of God, or when seek to uncover God's will for us. Certainly not. The word of God must be questioned constructively in order for it to be understood properly, and for its meaning to be applied to our lives and circumstances. History is full of the faulty interpretation of the word of God, and it has been used to justify all kinds of un-Christlike social and personal behavior. The unexamined word of God is not the word of God at all.

The point at issue for us is our immediate and joyful acceptance of the word of God. Understanding it properly is an issue of study, reflection, and prayer.

In the same way, it takes reflection and prayer to uncover God's will for each of us in the circumstances of our individual lives. Our Lord wants us to seek God's will as best we can, with a great desire to uncover it, and with a ready obedience to follow it when we find it.

We need to become modern-day Jeremiahs, coming to the kingdom and to its discipline as he came to the word of God. For all its discipline, and its cost to him personally, he came to accept the word with an enthusiastic heart: "When I found your words, I devoured them; they became my joy and the happiness of my heart, / Because I bore your name, O Lord, God of hosts" (Jeremiah 15:16).

139A Twenty-seventh Sunday in Ordinary Time

MATTHEW 21:33–43

God's Vineyard

The Bible has many images for the state of grace whereby God and His holy people live in harmony together. One image is the Promised Land, the land flowing with milk and honey. Another is God's pasture, where He shepherds His sheep by restful waters. A third is the one we hear in today's Gospel, the vineyard of God where the vines are full and fruitful. Nowadays, we apply all these images to the kingdom that Jesus established, and of which you and I are a part. The Gospel urges us to be worthy of it.

The image of the vineyard is found in Isaiah especially. And it is Isaiah's description of the vineyard that Jesus is drawing upon. The context in which Jesus spoke this parable is the continuing opposition to him by the chief priests and the Pharisees.

They know what Jesus is doing. He is condemning them. They are responsible to God for the care of his vineyard, Israel. But they have allowed its walls to be broken and breached by pagan alliances and by the incursion of false gods. They have rejected the prophets who were sent to them to challenge their indolence and to revive their sense of pastoral responsibility. In fact, they have beaten some, killed others, and stoned the rest. Now God has sent His Son to them. "They will respect my Son." But they don't. Our Lord confronts them with the awful truth that they are planning the Son's death.

Therefore, God's vineyard will be taken away from them and given to "a people that will produce its fruit." You and I have become the inheritors of God's taking away, on the one hand, and giving, on the other. We are, marvel of marvels, the new vineyard of the Lord! Such a gift, such a grace, and such a responsibility is ours!

The vineyard is the kingdom of God on earth. It is the Church, too, for the Church is the cutting edge of the kingdom. And it is your family and our parish. And it is your soul and my soul. In order to help us respond fruitfully, it is good to know that God trusts us to be responsible tenants. He has confidence in us. He will not take away our vineyard because of some weakness or mistake on our part. He understands those things. We will lose the vineyard only because of callous behavior, inexcusable indolence, and insincerity.

God does not demand perfection in our vineyard, but the heart to try for perfection. He does not demand fruitfulness based on our human efforts alone, but on his abounding grace enabling and multiplying our honest efforts. Nothing superhuman is required of us alone. We can take a page from John Steinbeck's novel *The Grapes of Wrath*. His novel is the modern retelling of the biblical story of the Promised Land and the vineyard of God.

When the Joad family reaches the California border and the edge of their promised land, after their trek from the dust bowl of the 1930s, they meet a stranger. He tells them what's ahead for them: "You never seen such purty country—all orchards an' grapes, purtiest country you ever seen. An' you'll pass lan' flat an' fine with water thirty feet down, an' that lan's layin' fallow." The only thing that the Joad family needs to do is to thank God for his laid-on gift and not leave it lying fallow. The only thing we need to do is cooperate with God's abounding grace.

142A Twenty-eighth Sunday in Ordinary Time

MATTHEW 22:1–14 (LONGER) OR MATTHEW 22:1–10 (SHORTER)

What the Busy Are Missing

The wedding feast here in the context of Matthew's Gospel is the gathering of believers in the kingdom of God, which Jesus inaugurated on earth. The kingdom is the great wedding feast that the Father put on for His Son, Jesus, and for which invitations were sent out. Once again, at issue is the rejection of Jesus by the primary invitees, the Jews.

Since they turn down the invitation, the Gentiles are invited in their place. "Go out, therefore, into the main roads and invite to the feast as many as you find." You and I are among these invited Gentiles.

The reference to the king sending his armies to destroy the ungrateful invitees and their city is Matthew's interpolation into the text. He is referring to the destruction of Jerusalem in 70 AD, which he (later) sees as a consequence of the Jews' rejection of Christ's wedding feast.

The reference to the guest who was thrown out because he was not wearing the wedding garment always seems to rub parishioners the wrong way. Throwing someone out just because he is not properly attired seems very harsh. But we must remember that when kings held wedding feasts they provided the wedding robes free. And they were costly regal robes, not a modern rented tux. A guest showing up without the wedding garment on, or with a soiled one (that is, having already worn it for some other purpose), was the height of insult. Hence the harsh but just treatment he received. We may interpret this to mean that we, who are the chosen and the abundantly graced guests of God, must not appear before God at the end with soiled souls.

How should we understand the line, "Some ignored the invitation and went away, one to his farm, another to his business"? Clearly, the Gospel is not condemning work and business. They are staples of normal life. The king is sad, not over the staples, but over the priorities. It is not every day that we are invited to a wedding feast, and there is no wedding invitation of greater import to us than that of taking our place in the kingdom of God. It is a unique invitation. It is *the* priority in our lives.

Well, here we are in our lovely country, all work and business, eyes glued to sales charts and ears anchored to cell phones. We are busily engaged in the necessary pursuits that the modern economy demands of us in the staples of life. But the staples are pushing us into the trap that William Barclay describes as being "so busy making a living that [we] fail to make a life." Many of us may be in that trap. Our priorities may have slowly changed from what they once were. Have the staples become the priorities? And we are so busy making a living that we no longer have a decent spiritual life? We are rushed and rattled from morning until night meeting workloads, deadlines, and bills by date due.

Consequently, there are casualties all over the Western world. Many one-time believers have lost the Lord's wedding feast invitation entirely. Some of us haven't, but we may be giving an ever-receding back seat to the kingdom of God in our lives. We know a degree of job satisfaction and financial satisfaction and football satisfaction and vacation satisfaction, but perhaps we feel in our bones that we are only living on the surface of the real meaning of life. Something is very wrong. Something is missing. What Julian Huxley saw happening to God "operationally" under the onslaught of science is now happening "operationally" in the Western mindset: "God is beginning to resemble not a ruler but the last fading smile of a cosmic Cheshire cat" *(Religion without Revelation)*.

Do we have that deep inner joy of the Christian who sits with Christ at the wedding feast? Or are we so busy that God and Christ and Church are joining that long list of nagging nuisances in our lives? Are we moving, as so many in the West in our time have moved, farther and farther away from any sense of the words of Francis of Assisi who said that God is someone to be enjoyed?

Let us ask God for the gift of deep inner joy in our lives. It is the wedding garment of those who know how to celebrate at the king's feast. Work gives satisfaction. Life gives pleasures. The kingdom of God gives the anchoring gift of inner peace and joy.

145A Twenty-ninth Sunday in Ordinary Time

MATTHEW 22:15–21

Giving God His Dues

The American Revolution patriot Thomas Paine wrote, "Government, even in its best state, is but a necessary evil" *(Common Sense)*. A British election slogan of 1976 read, "Every government should carry a health warning." Will Rogers once quipped, "I don't make jokes—I just watch the government and report the facts" (*The Saturday Review,* 8/25/1962).

On the other hand, the British statesman and writer Edmund Burke wrote, "Government is a contrivance of human wisdom to provide for human wants" ("Reflection on The French Revolution"). And the late Yale historians Will and Ariel Durant in their summary book, *The Lessons of History,* wrote that history has a good word to say "for government in general."

Government, in one form or another, seems to be a human necessity given our propensity to selfishness and abuse. I don't think any of us believe that Caesar, meaning the government, is altogether a bad thing. But most of us, I imagine, don't like to see too much of him.

Jesus says, "Then repay to Caesar what belongs to Caesar and to God what belongs to God." Fair enough. But is Caesar too demanding, as the Church was sometimes too demanding in the past? Probably. We could argue the case in several areas. Taxes are always and everywhere a bone of contention; so is intrusion into privacy. And the ease with which governments get themselves—and us—into silly wars or foreign policy minefields is yet another.

At any rate, the Lord enjoins us to give Caesar the lawful taxes that support the necessary public institutions and the many public services that benefit everyone. Saint Peter also reminds us of the Jewish tradition of praying for our public authorities (see 1 Peter 2:17). Let us give our Caesar both his taxes and our prayers.

And what of God's dues? We often subvert them in our dues to the Church. God and Church are not identical, and the one is not a stand-in for the other. Paying the priest's salary is not exactly paying God the worship that is His due! Our praise and prayer is. Pleasing the pastor is not a replacement for practicing the virtues and living the commandments! Fixing the church roof for free is no substitute for fixing your soul when it needs fixing!

Sometimes there can be a clash between what Caesar wants of us and what God wants of us. The clash is usually over moral issues. It is likely that we, in the age of rapid and increasing technology allied to weakening faith and little room for God in the scheme of things, will face more and more ethical issues where the law of God conflicts with Caesar's law. We who follow the Lord must follow the higher law of God when the state legalizes its opposite. What is legal is not always moral.

I don't believe that Jesus intended us to make God and Caesar equals in our allegiances, or in our hearts, or in our love, or in our services, or in our dues. God alone is God. There is no other. He commands the first and the best in us. Caesar, even committed to public service and with all His proper dues attached, is still only a pale shadow when placed in the light of God.

148A Thirtieth Sunday in Ordinary Time

MATTHEW 22:34–40

Giving God Priority Love

Last Sunday, the Gospel spoke of giving God and Caesar their dues. I said to you then that I did not believe that the Gospel equalized God and Caesar in our hearts or in the dues we owe them. Today, the Gospel speaks of God and neighbor and, I believe, it does not equalize the love that each is due from us.

In saying that, I know that I am swimming against the tide of popular opinion today. Concern for people is strong in our culture, and no one wishes to undermine that grace. After all, "faith of itself, if it does not have works, is dead" (James 2:17). And "if anyone says 'I love God,' but hates his brother, he is a liar; for whoever does not love a brother whom he has seen cannot love God whom he has not seen" (1 John 4:20). Nevertheless, you and I are not called by Christ to a Western humanitarianism devoid of God, nor does Christ call us to a law of love where God comes in second best in our services.

Jesus says, "You shall love the Lord, your God, with your whole heart. This is the great and the first commandment. The second is like it: You shall love your neighbor as yourself." There is a first and a second here.

I knew a young man who ran a service for indigent men. He was as dedicated to the urban poor as any person I have known. He came from a strong Catholic background. We were proud of him. One day he began to attack the clergy for every cent we spent on liturgical renewal for the worship of God. These monies, he claimed, were the pennies of the poor. God could take care of himself. This attitude infects all of us to a degree.

Christ was Jewish in his human origins. We are followers of Christ. In that Judeo-Christian theology, our priorities are set for us. God comes first. The neighbor comes second. The worship and love of God is our first service. The respect and love of the neighbor, in whom God images himself, follows logically. In the Church of recent years, God has sometimes been a poor second to the neighbor in our hearts. In the Western culture of charity, God is not present at all. The neighbor is everything.

Our love of neighbor issues from our prior love of God. If it does not, it will rest on foundations that are as flimsy and as changeable as our emotions and our economic circumstances. Giving on impulse is no substitute for giving with deep faith in God.

Saint Francis, "the poor man of Assisi," is perhaps the best loved saint of all. Millions throughout the world revere him for his love of the animals—but they do not love or worship the God who made both Francis and the animals. Millions of the unchurched bring their pets for the Church's blessing on his feast day—but they never ask for God's blessing on themselves. Millions admire the poor man of Assisi who kissed the lepers—but they do not acknowledge the God who inspired the poor man to kiss the lepers. Millions have disconnected the second commandment from the first. Millions of others have lost the first commandment entirely.

Are we in the modern Church to continue the disconnection? Saint Francis wrote in his *Rule for the Brothers,* "Whoever comes to us, friend or foe, thief or robber, should be received with kindness." Why? Not just because they fall under the general heading of neighbors. And not just to fulfill the law of humanitarianism; and not only because of human solidarity. And not just to love the people we can see without reference to the God we cannot see. Francis gives a frontal answer in his *Prayer Inspired by the Our Father:* "May we love our neighbors as ourselves, by drawing them all with our whole strength to the love of God."

151A Thirty-first Sunday in Ordinary Time

MATTHEW 23:1–12

On Not Trashing Religion

This is another teaching of Jesus sparked by the scribes' and the Pharisees' opposition to him. And, once again, in telling us what is wrong with them, he is telling us how to act correctly as his followers.

The scribes and the Pharisees occupy Moses' chair or teaching authority. That is, they are duly appointed teachers in Israel. Therefore, their teaching is to be obeyed. We may question the words attributed to Jesus: "Do and observe everything they say." These words seem contradictory here. Biblical scholar John P. Meier says that they may reflect "the early, stringently Jewish-Christian stage of Matthew's church" *(Matthew)*.

What did the scribes and the Pharisees teach? Basically, they taught the Law of God. However, according to Jesus in this Gospel passage, they added an extra burden of stringent interpretation, rules and regulations—and a religious attitude or mindset—that almost broke the backs of God's people. They turned the Law into legalism. In so doing, they buried the spirit of the covenant as something rich and satisfying between a loving God and His chosen people.

The word *Pharisee* comes from a Hebrew root meaning "separate." The Pharisees were "the separated ones" or "those who separate themselves" *(Oxford Dictionary of the Bible)*. They were separated, first of all, in choosing to be different from others, different even from the strictly orthodox Jews. And, secondly, they were separated in the sense that they came to differ from all others in their extreme and meticulous observance of each religious regulation. The doing became everything: the spirit suffered in consequence. These were the burdens they wished to place on other people's shoulders, and for which Jesus condemned them roundly. They brought religion into disrepute for all their desire to exalt it and to be its shining exponents.

If a pious Jew had followed the kind of religion the Pharisees trumpeted, he or she would have had ulcers, and no time for anything else in life, including work and home keeping. In the theological world of the Pharisees, God quickly becomes an overbearing taskmaster and religion becomes a soul-sapping slavery. So, when Jesus said, "Do everything and observe everything they tell you," we may assume that he wished people to do and observe what the duly appointed teachers in Israel should be teaching and doing—the Law of God in its covenant love.

What of the way we ourselves present and practice religion in the parish and in family life? Religion should be a salvation and a joy. Of course it has its challenges and its prohibitions but, at root, religion is a matter of salvation and of joy. Theologian William Barclay asks us to ask ourselves: Does our belief and practice help us or haunt us? Is our faith something with wings to lift us up or a weight to drag us down? May we never lose the spirit of our religion for its letter, nor become lost in too many regulations!

As for the Pharisees' piety, it was ultimately self-centered. Their myriad rules and regulations drove them in on themselves. They ended up doing "all their works to be seen by men," as Jesus said. Contrary to the Pharisees, Jesus wants our piety to be other-centered. As biblical scholar John P. Meier notes, "The Pharisees' self-centered piety closed them to genuine pastoral concern about others" (John P. Meier, *Matthew*).

All of us should be ready to serve others, be they neighbor or stranger, and not exclude them or separate ourselves from them. We should make the effort, without any sense of superiority or hint of ostentation, to be the servant of all. And in the stillness of our private prayer with God, we should be able to turn to Him and say from the depth of a humble and insightful heart that we are His servants and the servants of others doing "no more than our duty" (Luke 17:10).

154A Thirty-second Sunday in Ordinary Time

MATTHEW 25:1–13

On Not Being Too Late

The Church's liturgical year draws near its close, as it began, with a call to be ready for the final coming of Christ. "Those who were ready went into the wedding feast with him."

The function of the bridesmaids at a Jewish wedding was to keep the bride company until the groom arrived. When the groom's approach was announced, the bridesmaids were required to meet him and usher him into the bride's presence. The door was then shut. Once that happened, no one could be allowed in. The feast lasted a whole week in the house and it was, in fact, what we nowadays call the honeymoon. If a guest or a bridesmaid was not ready, then the consequences were socially embarrassing for that person.

For our Lord, the foolish bridesmaids are the Jewish people. They have missed the wedding feast by not recognizing Jesus as the groom; they have lost their place in the kingdom of God by rejecting his Messiah Son. They were unprepared.

What of us? By God's grace, we are in the kingdom of God here on earth. The bridegroom is about to come again to take us—this time—to the wedding feast of heaven. Are we ready for this second and final coming of Christ? If we are not, we become the five foolish bridesmaids.

I think it is obvious that our Lord spoke this parable with us in mind. It was too late for the people of Israel. They had missed the boat. So, why would he tell the story, except it be more as a warning to the future than a lament for the past? And note that it is something occupying his mind as his own life comes near its close.

It would be tragic for us to repeat Israel's mistake. It would be tragic for us to spend our lives in the kingdom of God on earth, in the Church for example, and yet miss the final chapter in the story of the kingdom and of salvation.

Some people rely on last-minute preparations, as the foolish ones in the Gospel parable did and had no oil ready in their lamps. I'm not a great believer in last-minute preparations. And I am not a great believer in death-bed conversions. I do not rule them out, of course, but they must be regarded by the sensible as infrequent graces. I do not believe that we should rely on what is the exception to the rule—"Betwixt the stirrup and the ground, mercy he sought, mercy found" (A. C. Swinburne). That is the exception. What is the rule? It is the Bible's assumption that our death will catch us in the way we normally live, be that as friend or enemy of God, and be it a prepared state or a postponed one. And, in this age of cars and commuting, we know from sad experience how quickly the end comes for many.

Jesus is "the treasure of all the nations"(Haggai 2:7). What a gift that he should have chosen you and me as the friends of the bridegroom! What a grace that he should have chosen us to prepare his wedding feast! What a joy that he should make us the modern counterparts of the five who were wise, and who await his glorious return so that we may go in with him to the eternal banquet!

This is our graced future. May we live each day worthily in its expectation.

157A Thirty-third Sunday in Ordinary Time

MATTHEW 25:14–30 (LONGER) OR MATTHEW 25:14–15, 19–21 (SHORTER)

Payback Time

It is possible to interpret this story in a number of ways. The one I want to place before you is this. Jesus is the man in the story. He is going away soon to heaven. He entrusts his property, the kingdom of God on earth, to the Church. We are the Church. He gives us talents and graces for expanding the kingdom on earth, for bringing others to personal salvation, and for bringing society under God's rule of love and peace and justice. He will return again, at the end, to gather the gains of his trust in us, and the gains of our investments on his behalf.

The first lesson we should learn from this story is not our Lord's condemnation of the Christian who does nothing with his or her talent, but our Lord's great trust in us. He has entrusted the work of salvation to us. We are, in Saint Paul's imagery, the hands and the mouth and the heart of Christ to others in our own time and place. Our talents and gifts are to be invested with them for the sake of Christ.

There is a second lesson. We are not all equally talented and equally gifted. Some of us are the servants of five talents, some of two, some of only one. It is, therefore, not an issue of how many talents we have but how responsible we are with whatever gift or grace that God gives us.

The third lesson is that the one who best serves the kingdom is one who will be asked to do even more. We are familiar with this phenomenon even in the workplace. The boss always gives more work to the one who gets things done. But this should not be seen as an imposition: it is a statement about output and trust and a promising future.

The fourth lesson is one about the fearful or the lazy servant. He has nothing to show for the talent given him. He is not punished because he invested the talent and gained no return on it, but because he just buried the talent in the ground. He did nothing at all with it.

Scholars tell us that the fearful or lazy servant with the one talent stands for the Pharisees. In Old Testament times, they were entrusted with God's Law. They did nothing salvific with it. They buried it in the ground in the sense that they killed its spirit with their legal minutiae. They fenced it around in the sense that they kept it from the people as if it were their own exclusive property. In their hands, God's Law was not invested with the people, and it did not yield any spiritual return.

Our lives and talents are opportunities for us to serve the Gospel and the kingdom. They are opportunities for investing ourselves in others' needs and hopes. Jesus has chosen us to bring his light and love to those around us. This servanthood of ours is not to be marked by fear and anxiety, or the fencing in and burial of gifts. This servanthood is a mark of God's favor to us, and of his graciousness to others through us.

May we, then, open up our faith with generosity. Surely it is enough for us to know that we are the chosen and the sufficiently talented servants of God and of others, in our own time and place in salvation history.

Solemnities during Ordinary Time

160A Last Sunday in Ordinary Time

Our Lord Jesus Christ the King
Thirty-fourth Sunday in Ordinary Time

MATTHEW 25:31–46

King of Hearts and Human Tatters

The king who invested his very life on us is the glorious King of kings and the Lord of lords of the final book of the Bible. All time is his, and all the seasons; all sovereignty is his, and eternal glory. And yet, our Lord chooses to describe himself as a king of hearts and a lord of love in the scene of final judgment, which is our Gospel for today.

If our Lord is the lord of love, then the Christian is called above all else to love the Lord and to love him in loving others for his sake. Our Gospel today could not possibly make any clearer the identity of you and me as lovers for Christ's sake, and of our Lord taking on the disguise of the people who cross our path. "*I* was hungry and you gave *me* food, when you gave it to the hungry on your doorstep and to the children of a distant famine. *I* was ill and you cared for *me*, when you visited your neighbor with cancer in the hospice. *I* was the stranger and it was *me* you welcomed, when you welcomed the strange asylum seeker on your street."

When someone dies—a politician, a bishop, a priest, a neighbor—I am not very interested in the eulogy that "celebrates" his or her life if that life was not one substantially marked by kindness, forgiveness, and a wide humanity. For, as the preface of the *Roman Catechism* states, "The whole concern of doctrine and its teaching must be directed to the love that never ends." And the *Catechism of the Catholic Church* notes in its treatment of the end—quoting Saint John of the Cross—"In the evening of life, we shall be judged on our love" (*Dichos de Luz y Amor*).

Theologian William Barclay tells this story. Saint Martin of Tours was a Roman soldier. One cold winter day, as he entered a city a beggar stopped him and asked for alms. Martin had no money, but the beggar was blue and shivering from the cold, and Martin gave what he had. He took off his soldier's cloak, and cut it in two, and gave half to the beggar. That night he had a dream. In it he saw the heavenly places and all the angels and Jesus among them, and Jesus was wearing half of a Roman soldier's cloak. One of the angels said to him, "Master, why are you wearing that battered old cloak? Who gave it to you?" And Jesus answered softly, "My servant Martin gave it to me."

One reality has always anchored me to the Christian faith in this world of many faiths and of none. It is the remarkable humanity of the Christian God. He came among us as a poor man. He spent his life doing all the good we would allow him to do, loving and lifting up the tattered humanity that crossed his path, and always spinning the seamless robe of love that was his poor man's life.

In the end, when all will be consummated, he will come in glory and as the King of kings and the Lord of lords. And yet, when he sits on his judgment seat, the judgment will be concerned only with what we continued to do for him, the poor man, as he did before us, with the tattered human lives that God placed along our pilgrim way.

Do we follow a king of glory or a king of tatters? Both, I suppose. We will find our glory, as he found his, in the tatters of others' lives.

164A The Most Holy Trinity

Sunday after Pentecost

JOHN 3:16–18

What's God Like Inside?

Most major football or baseball games or even golf tournaments these days are not complete without a sign behind the goal posts or home plate that reads either John 3:7 or John 3:16: "You must be born from above," or, "For God so loved the world that he gave his only Son, so that everyone who believes in him might not perish but might have eternal life." The sign is the missionary effort of Christian evangelicals who believe that those of us watching the game, be we the traditionally churched or not, and all the rest of the nation out there in TV land, badly need redemption.

Why is this Gospel chosen by our Church for Trinity Sunday? It doesn't mention the Trinity. Perhaps it's because all three persons of the Trinity are mentioned in the third chapter of John's Gospel from which today's short reading is taken.

The Trinity is not easy to understand. Maybe that's the reason why we say so little from the pulpit about this "most fundamental and essential teaching in the hierarchy of the truths of the faith" (*Catechism of the Catholic Church*, 234). Even Pope Pius XII admitted that the Trinity is a mystery that we cannot unveil in this life.

Well, we have to try to unveil something in this homily! So, what is the Trinity? Three persons in one God. Really? A denial of the first commandment, say orthodox Jews. (There's only one God and He is indivisible.) A bit of a contradiction, says mathematics. (Three into one won't go.) Saint Patrick demonstrated it as best he could with the shamrock: three leaves out of one stem forming one whole. (But his illustration never made it into any orthodox seminary textbook.)

We will never uncover the mystery—meaning, the full marvelous truth—of the Trinity but we can still appreciate it, if only in a veiled way. Some of our difficulty with the Trinity springs from the use of the word *person*. What *person* means in the theology of the Trinity is not what *person* means in common language. We make a mistake in looking at the three divine persons in God in the same way that we look at three human persons. There is a complete distinction between three human persons. They are three separate entities. The one is not the other, and cannot be.

A human person is an active, independent subject with his or her own *unique* subjectivity, knowledge, freedom, and life. The divine persons are not persons in that sense. If they were, they would be three Gods. So, the three divine persons are not persons in our sense. Each divine person is God, whole and entire, but there is only one God, because the distinction between them is only, if we may put it this way, in their relationship to one another, and in the tasks or operations that scripture ascribes to each one. They remain "the same God who produces all of them in everyone." (See 1 Corinthians 12:6.)

The Trinity actually tells us what God is like "on the outside" and "on the inside." On the outside, the creation and the redemption are clearly expressions of God's love as we see in the scriptures. So, we are able to know from these events that God "on the inside" must be a principle or dynamic of love. The Father, Son, and Spirit "personalize" that love.

The Trinity is a marvelous mystery of love. The Trinity is our way of talking about the inside and the outside of God. It's all about love and love's expressions, about God as endless depth of love in himself, and about God expressing this love in relationships with us. God's love becomes a trinity of expressions in the divine persons. They are community among themselves, and they push themselves outward as love and care and concern for us.

So, within Himself, God is a community of such "persons." God is family through these persons. This family structure of God is the source and template of the families we form on earth and of the communities we build. All of them image, in their own way, the divine community that is God.

When I look ahead to the death that increasingly beckons me with the passing of the years, I do not see myself passing on to some fearful and mysterious "beyond." I see myself going home. I will enter the heart of the divine family that formed me even before my mother's womb. My whole life has been directed by Trinitarian presences. My whole life on earth has been bonded together by God's communitarian form reflected in my natural family, my community of friends, the fraternity of priesthood, and the fellowship of Church that eased my journey through life. The family that is in God was the beginning point of my journey, and it remains the terminal point of my odyssey.

I will go "home" to God; home, because the Trinitarian God is a community of loving persons whose inner dynamic is love, and whose every word and action toward me has been that of a loving family working together for the child they created in their own image of love.

167A The Most Holy Body and Blood of Christ

Sunday after Trinity Sunday

JOHN 6:51–58

Why Go to Mass?

In some families today, the issue of Sunday Mass becomes the bone of contention. "Why do I have to go to Mass?" "I won't go!" "Stop pushing your religion down my throat!" Usual answer: "You'll do as you're told—at least for as long as you're under this roof!"

Sensitive parents sense their own failure in this rebellion. "What did we do wrong that makes them turn out this way?" Good parents shouldn't blame themselves. Rebellion, "kick against the goad" (Acts 26:14), is part of growing up, of "breaking away" as the title of a movie puts it. It is an understandable bid for freedom, a testing of the restraints as the adolescent tries for self-understanding and self-determination in that confusing process called the search for self-identity. It's all part of becoming a person. Sooner or later, if not as adolescents then as adults, all of us have to sift for ourselves the cultural and religious ways in which we were brought up, and come to reject them or to own them personally. That, in part, is what the kids are doing when they rebel over Mass.

Part of one's personal ownership of the Mass comes, I think, through an honest consideration of our Lord's words. Sunday Mass should have far more to do with what the Lord expects of those who love him than with parents' pressure and Church law. We cannot honestly say things like, "I am a Catholic but I don't go to Mass" or "I follow Christ, but forget this Eucharist business." I don't believe we can say such things with integrity. Why is that? Let us look at the Eucharist in the light of what Christ himself has said.

In today's Gospel he says, "Unless you eat the flesh of the Son of Man and drink his blood, you have no life in you." This is Christ speaking to us, not our parents or the Church. Fine. But how are we to understand these words? I believe we should understand them in the way those closest to the Lord understood them, and as the earliest generations of Christians understood them, and as the majority of believers down the Christian centuries have understood them: as the Eucharist.

The Eucharist is the memorial of Christ's sacrifice on Calvary. The Church understands memorial in a profound way. Mass is not just a memory of Calvary, a calling to mind of something long past: It is the making present now of that event in all its power and grace for us. In the Eucharist that we are attending in our parish church, "Christ gives us the very body which he gave up for us on the cross, the very blood which he 'poured out for many for the forgiveness of sins'" (*Catechism of the Catholic Church*, 1365).

This understanding of the memorial, of what he asked us to do in his memory, is not possible by simply praying alone in the privacy of one's room, or even by reading the account of it in the scriptures. Our presence and our participation in the memorial are required. I go to Mass for this reason.

In addition, for those who participate in the Eucharist, there is a pledge of future glory with Jesus. He said, "Whoever eats my flesh and drinks my blood has eternal life, and I will raise him on the last day." I go to Mass because of this pledge of the Lord himself.

There is more. I go to Mass because my Lord expects me to be there and, even, commands my presence. He said, "Take and eat; this is my body; take and drink; this is my blood." Then he said, "Do this in memory of me" (Luke 22:19). If I am a Christian, how can I ignore these commands of his? He said, "If you love me, you will keep my commandments" (John 14:15).

His introductory words to the eucharistic scene at the Last Supper are words of desire and of invitation: "I have eagerly desired to eat this Passover with you before I suffer" (Luke 22:15). These words of desire and of invitation are spoken not only to the first generation of his followers, but to all the generations of Christians, including you and me.

Saint Thomas Aquinas summarizes the value and the attraction of the Eucharist. He calls it a sacred banquet, in which Christ is received; in which his suffering and death are recalled (that is, re-enacted); through which we are filled with God's grace; and because of which we are given the pledge of future glory in heaven. An awful lot is riding on the Eucharist and on our participation in it! (See *O Sacrum Convivium.*)

The Eucharist is too central to Christ's heart for any Christian to ignore it. It is too rich in grace for us to avoid it. Our appreciation of it cannot be left to our parents' urging or to the Church's legislation. We have to grow up and outgrow them. The Eucharist is the Christian's own responsibility before Christ, and because of his invitation. And it is the mature Christian's deepest joy.

622 The Assumption of the Blessed Virgin Mary

August 15 / Solemnity Mass during the Day

LUKE 1:39–56

Our Pattern

The late John Denver wrote "Annie's Song." Today's Gospel gives us "Mary's Song," the Magnificat. She did not compose all of it herself. Much of it is known as "Hannah's Song" among Jewish people. Mary used it as a praise prayer in gratitude to God when Elizabeth, inspired of the Spirit, exclaimed, "Blessed are you among women and blessed is the fruit of your womb."

We already see in this prayer the main strands of the Beatitudes that Jesus would later set as the foundation document of the kingdom of God and of the Church.

Mary is declaring herself a beatitude person. She is the servant of the Lord. She is the lowly one. She is one of "the poor ones of God," the cherished *anawim* of Israel. She is fully open to the will of God and fully reliant on the providence of God. She is not only filling with the infant in her womb; she is already full of faith and trust in God.

In the recent past, Mary's holiness and her virginity were
stressed in a way that may have seemed to distance her from us.
There was more than a little too much of other-worldliness about her.
She was our mother to be sure, and we could approach her on that
basis; but many of us did not see her exactly as a sister traveler, as
a pilgrim on the journey of a sometimes messy life and the journey of
a sometimes severely stretched faith. She was "up there" basically and
we were "down here."

The Second Vatican Council has balanced the matter for us.
Mary remains all that the Church ever said she is; but the Council has
brought her closer to our ecumenical concerns and, above all, closer
to us as a pilgrim who once walked our dusty way and is thereby a real-
life pattern for us and for our pilgrimage.

Vatican II begins its treatment of Mary (in cp. 8 of *Lumen
gentium*) immediately after its treatment of the Church as a pilgrim.
It tells us straightaway that Mary, like us, is one of the redeemed,
even if redeemed "in a more exalted fashion." She is one of us.
She is our "outstanding model in faith and charity." She was a pilgrim
as we are pilgrims, and she was the Lord's servant as we are called
to be. She was singular in the way that, as pilgrim and as servant, she
"cooperated [with God's saving will] by her obedience, faith, hope
and burning charity."

Assumed into heaven on the completion of her earthly life,
Mary is "a sign of certain hope and comfort to the pilgrim people of
God." Mary was assumed in glory at the end of her exemplary servant
pilgrimage on earth. Are we "assuming," that is, taking upon ourselves,
the attitudes and the virtues that characterized her pilgrim way so
that we, one day, will be assumed into the everlasting glory of heaven?
Mary is every Christian's pattern for the pilgrim way, and for the
assumption that completes it.

667 All Saints

November 1 / Solemnity

MATTHEW 5:1–12A

Our Heroes

About the last thing most people want to be known as is a saint.
To them it means a holy Joe, a pious Mary, someone out of touch, a bit
odd. Western culture is death on sanctity. Political correctness urges
us to adopt a more commonplace and anonymous humanity.

Hagiographers of the past, the people who wrote the lives
of the saints, are much to blame for the poor image saints have in the
popular mind. Saints were often presented as anti-human ascetics
and miracle workers. They appeared on the pages as anti-intellectual
and slightly irrational beings, or dripping with questionable theology
and psychological quirks. Sometimes, the very language that tried
to highlight their extraordinariness only increased their distance from
us. Hence, the wisdom of the world places sanctity beyond the pale
of a full and integrated humanity. It's only for oddities.

Saints are in need of rehabilitation. They are models to be
imitated, not freaks to be avoided.

Saints are, first of all, truly human men and women. That is
the first requirement in the process of canonization. Oddities are ruled
out on Rome's first page. Then Rome looks at what grace has done
with their human nature, following the axiom that "grace builds on
nature." Rome finds that they are not unusual or unique or in a different
class from the rest of us as to their human nature. They are who
we are, and they do what we do—but in an outstanding way. Why?
Because of their full cooperation with God's grace. Our saints are
simply the brothers and sisters who arrived at what our Lord wishes
for all of us, a true and full and graced humanity. It is called wholeness
or holiness. Saint Paul expresses it this way: "But grace was given
to each of us according to the measure of Christ's gift . . . until we all

attain to the unity of faith and knowledge of the Son of God, to mature manhood, to the extent of the full stature of Christ" (Ephesians 4:7, 13).

Our saints are heroes. They are the Christian's heroes. And if the world had a better wisdom and a deeper insight, it would come to realize that the saints are humanity's heroes as well. The saints enflesh that self-control, human integration, growth, and maturity that psychology and society struggle with and long for in all of us. If all were saints, the poor world would finally be rid of its violence, abuse, poverty, envy, and fragmentation.

Unfortunately, our culture does not model itself on the saints. Instead it names a street or a public housing project after them. Whatever the good intention of this, the saints are thereby consigned to what is past tense and merely monumental. Nineteenth-century British author Saki (Hector Hugh Munro) noted a similar but even worse fate for saints in the Britain of a century ago, "their names . . . associated nowadays chiefly with racehorses and the cheaper clarets" *(Reginald at the Carlton).*

The saints are the men and women that the Church puts before us as outstanding models of humanity and of Christian discipleship. They are living scriptures. If you were unable to read a Bible but lived with a saint, you could read God's word and walk God's way by the light of the life of that saint. The Church puts them in front of our faces as guideline, model, pattern, encouragement, and hope in our own struggle for discipleship, integrity, and Christian fullness.

689 The Immaculate Conception of the Blessed Virgin Mary

December 8 / Solemnity

LUKE 1:26–38

Mary's Necessary Grace

The Immaculate Conception is the teaching that Mary was conceived in her mother's womb untouched by original sin. The stain that marks every human being born into this world did not touch her. She is, as the poet wrote, "our tainted nature's solitary boast." This was a grace given to Mary such as was given to no one else. Why? Because of the vocation God had chosen for her. She was to conceive and bring forth the world's Savior. It would be inappropriate for the Savior to be born of a woman who was herself stained by sin.

This gift of Mary's Immaculate Conception should be seen as something not of her own doing, and not for herself alone, but as Pius IX named it, "a singular grace and privilege of Almighty God" given to Mary through the future "merits of Jesus Christ." It is a grace won for her—in advance, so to speak—on Calvary. Above all, it is a grace given to her on our behalf, for our salvation.

Mary's greatness and her gifts must never be divorced from God's saving plan for us. All of her gifts and privileges are from God. All are due to the merits of her Son, and relate, in one way or another, to God's plan of salvation for us.

Mary's personal greatness, for me, is in the way she cooperated wholeheartedly with God's will and His gifts and privileges to her. Thus, she is our primary model of the Christian way of life after, of course, her Son. One virtue of Mary stands out in the Gospels. It is her dedication to doing God's will. When she calls herself "the hand-maid [or servant] of the Lord," she expresses that service as the free and complete harmony of her will with God's will. With Mary, it's always a matter of "let it be done to me as you say."

And so, it doesn't surprise me at all that her Son, more than thirty years on, will gather his disciples around him and teach them the content of the servant's prayer. He will teach them to begin the prayer with the traditional Jewish greeting of God, "Hallowed be thy name." That done, they are to say to him, "May thy kingdom come, and may thy will be done on earth as it is done in heaven."

Mary is our model for many aspects of the Christian life, but particularly, I feel, our model of the servant always seeking God's will and doing it.

About the Liturgical Institute

The Liturgical Institute, founded in 2000 by His Eminence Francis Cardinal George of Chicago, offers a variety of options for education in Liturgical Studies. A unified, rites-based core curriculum constitutes the foundation of the program, providing integrated and balanced studies toward the advancement of the renewal promoted by the Second Vatican Council. The musical, artistic, and architectural dimensions of worship are given particular emphasis in the curriculum. Institute students are encouraged to participate in its "liturgical heart" of daily Mass and Morning and Evening Prayer. The academic program of the Institute serves a diverse, international student population—laity, religious, and clergy—who are preparing for service in parishes, dioceses, and religious communities. Personalized mentoring is provided in view of each student's ministerial and professional goals. The Institute is housed on the campus of the University of St. Mary of the Lake/Mundelein Seminary, which offers the largest priestly formation program in the United States and is the center of the permanent diaconate and lay ministry training programs of the Archdiocese of Chicago. In addition, the University has the distinction of being the first chartered institution of higher learning in Chicago (1844), and one of only seven pontifical faculties in North America.

For more information about the Liturgical Institute and its programs, contact: usml.edu/liturgicalinstitute. Phone: 847-837-4542. E-mail: dmcnamara@usml.edu.

Msgr. Reynold Hillenbrand
1904-1979

Monsignor Reynold Hillenbrand, ordained a priest by Cardinal George Mundelein in 1929, was Rector of St. Mary of the Lake Seminary from 1936 to 1944.

He was a leading figure in the liturgical and social action movement in the United States during the 1930s and worked to promote active, intelligent, and informed participation in the Church's liturgy.

He believed that a reconstruction of society would occur as a result of the renewal of the Christian spirit, whose source and center is the liturgy.

Hillenbrand taught that, since the ultimate purpose of Catholic action is to Christianize society, the renewal of the liturgy must undoubtedly play the key role in achieving this goal.

Hillenbrand Books strives to reflect the spirit of Monsignor Reynold Hillenbrand's pioneering work by making available innovative and scholarly resources that advance the liturgical and sacramental life of the Church.